RISING FROM ASHES

A Christ-Centered Smoking Cessation Program

JIM MORELAND

WESTBOW
PRESS®
A DIVISION OF THOMAS NELSON
& ZONDERVAN

Copyright © 2018 Jim Moreland.

All rights reserved. No part of this book may be used or reproduced by any means, graphic, electronic, or mechanical, including photocopying, recording, taping or by any information storage retrieval system without the written permission of the author except in the case of brief quotations embodied in critical articles and reviews.

WestBow Press books may be ordered through booksellers or by contacting:

WestBow Press
A Division of Thomas Nelson & Zondervan
1663 Liberty Drive
Bloomington, IN 47403
www.westbowpress.com
1 (866) 928-1240

Because of the dynamic nature of the Internet, any web addresses or links contained in this book may have changed since publication and may no longer be valid. The views expressed in this work are solely those of the author and do not necessarily reflect the views of the publisher, and the publisher hereby disclaims any responsibility for them.

Any people depicted in stock imagery provided by Getty Images are models, and such images are being used for illustrative purposes only. Certain stock imagery © Getty Images.

THE HOLY BIBLE, NEW INTERNATIONAL VERSION®, NIV® Copyright © 1973, 1978, 1984, 2011 by Biblica, Inc.® Used by permission. All rights reserved worldwide.

Scripture taken from the New King James Version®. Copyright © 1982 by Thomas Nelson. Used by permission. All rights reserved.

ISBN: 978-1-9736-2614-5 (sc)
ISBN: 978-1-9736-2613-8 (hc)
ISBN: 978-1-9736-2615-2 (e)

Library of Congress Control Number: 2018904514

Print information available on the last page.

WestBow Press rev. date: 4/27/2018

CONTENTS

Acknowledgements vii
Dr. Lori Brister Deemer M.d. ix
Autumn's Testimony xi
Dedication xiii
Introduction xv

Chapter 1   How Jesus Delievered Me From Smoking
            Cigarettes 1
Chapter 2   Denial, Powerlessness, And Turning It Over
            To Christ 7
Chapter 3   The Risk Of Smoking And The Benefits Of
            Quitting/Nicotine Withdrawl And Gravings 13
Chapter 4   My Personal Battle To Quit Smoking 19
Chapter 5   Ephesians 4:22-24: Put-Offs/Put-Ons/
            Unforgiveness/Setting Goals 23
Chapter 6   Trusting In God's Strength 1 Samuel 17:1-51 35
Chapter 7   Accountability Teams Ecclesiastics 4:9-12 45
Chapter 8   God's Love Matthew 11:28-30 49
Chapter 9   Putting On The Whole Armor Of God
            Ephesians 6:10-17 57
Chapter 10 Perseverance Nehemiah Chapters 4&6 67
Chapter 11 Maintaining A Smoke Free Life 77

Final Lesson 79
Conclusion 85
Bibliography 87

ACKNOWLEDGEMENTS

There have been many Christian brothers and sisters that have encouraged, and helped me along the way in the Rising from Ashes (RFA) ministry. I want to acknowledge a few of them who have been instrumental in helping grow this ministry.

I want to thank my brother in Christ Scott, who has been one of my leaders since the beginning of Rising from Ashes.

I want to thank my sister in Christ Autumn. Autumn brought not only her enthusiasm to the ministry but her ability to gather professional speakers to speak to the class about issues that many smokers, during the process of quitting, encounter.

I want to thank my church family, at White River Friends in Winchester, Indiana, for their prayers and support.

Most importantly, I want to thank my Lord and Savior Jesus Christ, for redeeming me; a lost soul!

DR. LORI BRISTER DEEMER M.D.

Rising from Ashes is a Word inspired program designed to help people break free from the chains of nicotine addiction. The Lord designed us to live freely and to serve Him, being a slave to nothing. Smoking damages our physical bodies and our ability to carry out our earthly ministry. Our bodies are designed to begin healing the damage caused by smoking within hours of the last cigarette. It is truly amazing!

Jesus asked the man who had been lame for 38 years lying beside the pool of Bethesda hoping to get in and be healed, "Do you want to be well?" The skills and Scriptures provided through RFA are powerful, practical, and possible! I would encourage anyone who is sick and tired of being shackled by the chains of nicotine addiction, no matter how long those shackles have been on you, to come check it out. The healing pool is right beside you, so the question is, "Do you want to be well?" If so, take advantage of this wonderful ministry based upon God's healing Word. - Dr. Lori Brister Deeemer M.D.

AUTUMN'S TESTIMONY

I started smoking when I was twelve years old. I like to think that tobacco had always been in my body. My mother smoked when she was pregnant with me, and both of my parents smoked very heavily in the house and car. At first, I smoked more out of curiosity than anything; but by the time I was fifteen I was a half a pack a day smoker. I smoked for over twenty years.

When I was thirty-five, I learned that I was pregnant with our second child. Unlike my mother, I did not smoke while pregnant. I was working for a company that gave a great incentive to quit smoking for one year. I decided with nine months covered with the pregnancy, I could probably do another three. My mentality was that I would probably go back to smoking after about fourteen or fifteen months. I didn't actually believe that I would be able to quit for good.

One of the company requirements for the incentive involved completing a smoking cessation class put on by the hospital. When I started this class, I had already been smoke-free for five months. I walked into that class with the attitude that there was nothing they could tell me that had not been lectured to me over and over again. To my surprise, I gained fascinating information regarding my health. It also introduced the idea that nicotine was an addiction.

This was a big blow to me. Addiction! I saw it as a bad habit, a crutch, a less than desirable act in my life. Addiction is a nasty word. I had felt the sting of addiction before through a loved one, and I didn't want to be that person, an addict. Despite my feelings regarding the words addiction and addict, the more I learned, the more I realized that while I might not think of myself as an addict, the reality was that I fit that label.

With only a few classes to complete, my father started to struggle with COPD. I watched my father struggle to breath. During our Christmas celebration he had a severe coughing fit and passed out in front of everyone. On my way home, I looked at my husband, and said, "I am going to do anything and everything I can to make sure I do not develop COPD. I never want my kids to witness that kind of incident.

Around the same time, my church had announced the start of the Rising from Ashes class. I wrestled with the idea to go to such degree I missed the first class entirely. My desire to overcome addiction won out and I walked into all the other classes very pregnant.

RFA taught me to hand my burdens over to God. My burdens? God wants my burdens (cf. Matthew 11:28)? I had always felt like my problems were insignificant, and I had no right to ask God for anything. There were huge problems in the world and I shouldn't bother Him with mine.

The Rising from Ashes ministry showed me a whole new world; from giving my worries to God, to trusting in God, to knowing when I was under attack from the enemy. I didn't just stop smoking; "I became a whole new person." My life changed for me so much, because I learned how to rely on God. I was afraid to quit smoking, because I was afraid of what life would be like not being a smoker. But without fail, God showed me that my life would be nothing like I could imagine, if I would just trust Him.

DEDICATION

This book is dedicated to those who have lost their lives to cancer and other diseases caused by smoking cigarettes. And to those who are struggling today with serious diseases caused by cigarette smoke and other harmful tobacco products. Lastly, to remind those who are struggling today with smoking related diseases that it is never too late to quit.

INTRODUCTION

The addiction to cigarette smoking and other nicotine products robs God's people of their health and financial resources, which are essential in reaching the lost for Christ. It's often difficult for pastors and other ministry leaders, who know very little about nicotine addiction, to address this problem. My hope is that this book will help pastors and other church leaders understand the magnitude of nicotine addiction, within the church, and the need to address this issue in a biblical way.

In today's society, Smoking/chewing/vaping has become an accepted part of American culture. However, God's word is clear. God does not want His people to be in bondage to nicotine addiction or dependent on anything other than Him. Is smoking a sin? Is being addicted to smokeless tobacco, or inhaling nicotine through an electronic means a sin. Simply put; Yes! Before you get angry and slam this book shut, please, hear me out. It's made clear in Scripture that the Holy Spirit lives inside of God's children, "Do you not know that you are the temple of God and *that* the Spirit of God dwells in you" (1 Cor. 3:16, italics theirs). That verse clearly proclaims to us that the Holy Spirit lives inside of each individual Christian. The Holy Spirit represents the very presence of the Lord Jesus Christ taking up residence in your heart, and whatever you do to your body affects Jesus. Even if you don't agree that the addiction to nicotine is a sin the foundational verse of Rising from Ashes clears the air. God's desire is for all of His children to be free of any chains that bind them, "All things are lawful for me, but all things are not helpful. All things are lawful for me, but I will not be brought under the power of any" (1 Corinthians 6:12).

That Scripture speaks volumes to the question, should I use tobacco products? We have boundless freedom in Christ. Nicotine addiction, by itself, is not going to keep you out of heaven, but someday when we give an account of our lives to Christ we will have to give justification on what we did with the spiritual gifts we received, and how well we cared for the temple which Christ dwells in.

Rising from Ashes is a Christ-centered smoking cessation program designed to assist God's people in breaking the shackles of nicotine addiction and do it in a way that is not threatening or condemning to them. Rising from Ashes is based on the truths found in Scripture, solid biblical teachings, practical homework, and Scripture reading assignments. It's necessary for participants to take an active role in putting-off this addiction in order to reap the benefits.

It's important to complete the full process set forth in this book. From what I have observed at the end of each workshop the percentages of those who completed the process, thus becoming smoke free, are greatly increased compared to those who didn't finish the entire workbook. Secondly, I urge you not to make this about yourself; although, you will reap many benefits when you are nicotine free. Make it about pleasing Jesus! Make it about those you love and those who love you: children, grandchildren, spouse, mom and dad. There seems to be more motivation for success when we do something for the ones we love, and for the health and well-being of others than for our own well-being.

I also urge you to go through this process within the confines of a small group environment. Seek out other Christians around you that smoke and have a desire to quit. Than meet together once a week and go through this process. It's important, through this process, to build an accountability team and get support from others. A small group can help tremendously with that. I also believe that going through this process on your own will be beneficial and that you can find freedom from smoking.

This process consists of seven weekly assignments, with seven being the biblical number for completion. If you complete it sooner, ok, but complete each lesson before moving on to the next one. Do all reading assignments, thoroughly answer all questions, meet with your accountability person, and memorize the assigned Scriptures.

The facts are overwhelming that tobacco products injure and kill thousands every year. "Cigarettes kill more Americans than alcohol, car accidents, suicide, AIDS, homicide, and illegal drugs combined." (American Cancer Society)

My purpose for this book is to bring the truth of God's Word into the battle against nicotine addiction; bringing deliverance from this bondage to God's people.

Chapter 1

HOW JESUS DELIEVERED ME FROM SMOKING CIGARETTES

After forty years of smoking cigarettes, God delivered me from this expensive and deadly habit. I have no real writing experience; except, after falling in love, for the first time, when I was ten years old I wrote some very mushy, but what I felt, were some award-winning, heart-felt, and poetic words of my true love for the prettiest girl in Harris Elementary.

Given that disclaimer, this is my first attempt at writing about my experience, as a smoker. Worst of all, I discovered I was unable to overcome this habit on my own. I thought it would be good to start at the beginning. During our youthful years we often make life-changing decisions that we truly regret later in life. Those foolish decisions can cause many heart-aches for ourselves and others we love as we travel through this crazy mixed-up thing called life. I made several poor decisions while growing up and smoking cigarettes was one of those poor decisions.

Many poor decisions start innocently enough. Both of my parents smoked, so smoking was an accepted part of my home life and an accepted part of society during my youth. It was not uncommon to see cigarette ads on TV, billboards, in magazines, and hear them blaring on the radio. In general, the public, in those days, knew very little about the hazards cigarette smoking caused to themselves and to others. Smoking was portrayed as a cool, manly thing to do for men. If you have ever had the opportunity to see an old advertisement featuring the Marlboro man, you will better comprehend what I am talking about.

For the ladies, who were on the verge of a historic fight for women's rights in the sixties; smoking was a sign of freedom from the humdrum life of being a house wife. Smoking, for a woman, became a sign of sophistication, independence, and a way to slim down. Virginia Slim's ads from those times clearly portray smoking as a sign of maturity.

Smoking ads were designed in a way to entice you into trying tobacco products that the tobacco companies knew would harm you and eventually get you addicted to nicotine. It was a much simpler time, all those years ago, and no one really believed that large tobacco companies or the U.S. government would promote something that would be harmful to the citizens of this great nation. Hind sight being twenty-twenty! We, as citizens of this great country, have come to realize that when it comes to power and money, neither, corporations or governments are exempt from self-serving policies and actions.

My first experience with smoking cigarettes came about innocently enough. I was not lured to smoking through an exotic commercial, nor was I enticed by peer pressure, but through my sister, Mary, and her friend. My sister was thirteen months older than I was and much cooler; I wore big, thick glasses that looked like I was wearing the bottoms of a Coca-Cola bottle. I was shy and very self-conscious of my short comings. I want to share a very hurtful reality in my young life, so you can understand my mind-set at that time.

My childhood was a very lonely place. I lived in a neighborhood with no children my own age to play with. I hated school. I was constantly made fun of because I wore thick glasses. To add more grief to my situation, dad was a womanizer, and was gone most of the time leaving mom home alone to raise four kids. However, given my dad's tendency to smack me around and call me names, this was really a blessing in disguise.

I never really understood my dad, but he must have been a very unhappy person himself to cause so much grief for those he was supposed to love and protect. My mom was as much a victim of my dad's anger as were my sisters and I, and after twenty years of marriage mom, finally got the nerve to get a divorce.

I'm not complaining as I look back on those years. Even as hurtful as my childhood was, these experiences made me stronger. I had one goal as a young boy growing up, and that was to get big enough to "kick the tar" out of my dad. That never came about, and I forgave my dad many, many years ago and I pray I will see him in heaven someday.

The downright hatred I felt towards my dad damaged me through the years, and damaged my relationships with those around me. Many poor decisions I made over the years and the addictive behaviors I developed were directly related to my anger. Anger is a powerful emotion and can be used in a righteous way to inspire an individual to address an injustice; or, it can be used in a destructive way that eats at a person's soul and damages their physical, emotional, and mental health.

Even the Lord Jesus got angry at times. After entering the temple in Jerusalem, where people were buying and selling goods in God's house; Jesus got angry. Jesus, in no uncertain terms, let the merchandizers know that God's house was meant to be a sanctuary of prayer, not a shopping mall. Jesus, after turning the tables over and running the sellers out of the temple opened the temple doors to those who needed healing and a touch from God.

The Bible teaches us that we are not to let the day end in a state of anger. In other words, we should resolve our anger issues now. If you are harboring sinful anger, you need to get rid of it by repenting, forgiving others, and turning it over to God. Unresolved anger will hinder your spiritual growth and your ability to grow in Christ-likeness. Spiritual growth is essential for breaking the chains of nicotine addiction and discovering the glorious freedom we have been given in Christ.

Back to the first time I smoked cigarettes. Picking up that first cigarette started innocently enough for me. On a beautiful fall day (I remember the corn was brown and ready to be harvested) I was around ten years old when my sister Mary and her friend invited me to go smoke a cigarette with them. I was not at all interested in smoking cigarettes, but I was interested in my sister's friend. I went along with the smoking idea with the hope of impressing my sister's cohort in this juvenile crime, but it didn't work. My coughing and hacking didn't leave much of a "cool dude" impression on her. Mary's friend was obviously more interested in smoking than in me.

Sneaking off to smoke cigarettes became a regular thing for my sister and her friends, and on occasion I went along. Soon, I started smoking on my own. It was easy to purchase cigarettes back then. All you had to do was tell the clerk they were for your mom or dad and they sold them to you without question. I'm not blaming my cigarette addiction on Mary, her friends, or anyone else: I chose to smoke, and I need to take responsibility for that bad decision.

Young people are easily influenced by what they see their parents and grandparents do. Ask yourself this question, what impression will I be leaving on the young people I encounter that see me smoking? Every time you light up a cigarette think about the affect it's having on the young people around you. Let that thought build on your resolve to quit smoking.

I feel compelled to mention my other sisters, Dixie and Nancy, in this book to keep myself out of hot water with them. Dixie was a few years older than me and Nancy was a couple of years younger than me. Mary and I were closer in age and, because we had a lot more in common, we hung out together more. I love all of my sisters very much, I'm happy to say that we are all followers of Jesus Christ and former cigarette smokers.

As the years went by, cigarette smoking got a real strangle hold on me and no matter how hard I tried, I couldn't win the battle against this awful addiction. I soon began to realize how much those harmful chemicals in cigarette smoke were affecting my health. I was turning fifty years old, and it became challenging for me to walk the two hundred yards to the barn and back. After returning to the house, I was out of breath and wheezing. It was so frightening to me, after only a short walk I was left struggling for the very "breathe of life" God had given to me.

After trying and failing several times to quit, I was overwhelmed with feelings of hopelessness. Finally, after many years of struggling, I surrendered to this awful addiction: I came to the horrifying conclusion that cigarette smoking was going to kill me and there was nothing I could do about it.

A life changing miracle happened around that same time; I surrendered my life to Jesus Christ. One thing I have learned through the years is that Jesus is the one who transforms lives, and He began to transform mine. Right away there were many sins and destructive habits the Lord delivered me from, but the hopelessness of nicotine addiction held on to me like contact cement. No matter how bad I needed to quit smoking; I couldn't. When sharing my new-found faith with others, I began to feel convicted about my nicotine addiction. How could I tell others that Christ could set them free, when the truth was, I was struggling with an awful addiction that was killing me?

I had not planned on another miracle to happen in my life, but on July 3, 2000, Jesus Christ delivered me from smoking cigarettes, and I haven't smoked a cigarette since that day (complete details, of this miracle, are in chapter 4: my personal testimony, so, keep reading). I knew that only through the power of Christ could such a great deliverance happen. I realized at that very moment, within the confines of my heart, that Christ has the power to deliver folks from this awful addiction of cigarette smoking. I want to shout it from the hilltops, to all of you who read this book that Jesus set me free from nicotine addiction and Jesus wants to set you free too! After this awesome deliverance, the question I kept asking myself, for the next few years, was can a program, based on the power of Christ living in us, enable, God's people, who want to quit smoking, to quit?

The purpose for this book is to share with you a process that the Lord Jesus took me through, which lead up to the day I smoked my last cigarette. This book shares a Christ-centered smoking cessation program based on the truth and power of God's Word. The Rising from Ashes program was designed specifically to set the people of God free from the addiction to nicotine, but I feel strongly, even, if you haven't surrendered your life to Christ that this book will help you. The program that follows is based on biblical principles, the Scriptures, practical work assignments, and the truth found in the Word of God.

Chapter 2

DENIAL, POWERLESSNESS, AND TURNING IT OVER TO CHRIST

From the time I gave my life to Christ on February 13, 2000, until the time I quit smoking on July 3, 2000, the Lord, without me realizing it, took me through a three step process that led to the miracle deliverance from cigarettes, I experienced. Upon surrendering my life to Jesus, I felt compelled to help others with chemical addictions. Not only did smoking hold me captive for close to forty years alcohol enslaved me for nearly as long. Being a prisoner of those horrible addictions fed my desire to help others who were struggling. After meeting with my pastor, I enrolled in a biblical counseling course. Upon graduating from that course I got involvement in a Christ-centered recovery program called, "Celebrate Recovery" at Brandywine Community Church in Greenfield, IN. As I began to gain knowledge of the recovery process; I soon came to the realization that Jesus took me through the first three crucial steps of recovery, which led directly to breaking the chains of nicotine addiction that had me bound for so long.

The first recovery principle is to come out of denial. Denial, in no uncertain terms, is defined as "lying to self." Are humans proficient at deceiving themselves? James wrote, "But be doers of the word and not hearers only, deceiving yourselves" (James 1:22): if we read the Word of God, and don't do what it instructs us to do, we are only deceiving ourselves. Our lives will not change until we apply what we learn from Scripture into our everyday lives. That's a key during this process: applying the principles found in the Word of God to our everyday lives: "working the power of the Scriptures."

Since the fall of mankind, humans, because of sin, have been great liars especially to themselves. Denial is fear based; it's a fear of change. If I admit my denial, then I will have to change something in my life. When God came looking for Adam, in the Garden of Eden, Adam hid himself from God, because of fear, "Then the Lord God called to Adam and said to him, "Where are you." So he said, "I heard Your voice in the garden, and I was "afraid" because I was naked; and I hid myself" (Gen. 3:9-10 emphasis mine).

Are you trying to hide from God? Is he continuously whispering in your ear that it's time to quit smoking? Don't hide from God in a sea of denial. Instead, admit your denial and give Jesus the opportunity to set you free from the bonds of nicotine addiction. Denial is a false belief that keeps you from admitting you need to change a destructive habit in your life. Denial has been defined as, "A false system of beliefs that are not based on reality and a self-protecting behavior that keeps us from honestly facing the truth." - John Baker, Celebrate Recovery Leadership Guide

Have you been lying to yourself about smoking or the use of other nicotine products? What kind of lies have you been telling yourself and others? I can quit anytime! Once addicted to nicotine, it's very difficult to quit on your own. I'm not hurting anyone else! Second hand smoke kills thousands every year. It relaxes me! Cigarette smoking increases heart rate and blood pressure. I hope these lies of denial unraveled by the truth will help you make a list of your own denials and replace them with the known truths about tobacco use. Make a list of some of the lies you have used in the past to justify smoking. Then replace them with the truth found, through empirical research and in God's Word.

I can quit anytime I want! How many times have you told yourself that? The truth is that nicotine is one of the strongest addictions a person can have. As far back as 1987, the New York

Times Magazine, in an article, said, "Quitting the nicotine habit is harder to quit than heroine." I tried to quit several times on my own power, but after a short time, I went right back to smoking again. The desire to smoke was even stronger after I had stopped smoking for a while. It seemed I was powerless over this addiction. It took me totally surrendering this addiction to God before I was able to quit once and for all.

As difficult as it is to come out of denial it's equally difficult to admit our powerlessness. Since the fall of humankind, man has had a propensity to do the wrong thing: to feed his own ego and flesh. Adam and Eve wanted to be like God (Pride). That's why Adam and Eve ate fruit from the tree that God clearly told them not to eat of (cf. Gen. 2:17, 18). In the Garden of Eden, Satan countered God's truth with his lie. Sadly, Adam and Eve believed the devils lies instead of the truth of God's Word.

From that moment on, human-beings began a life of denial. Creating in them a false belief that they could handle sin on their own: I don't need any help; I can do this on my own! I'm human, hear me roar! Does that sound familiar? The truth is that humankind, apart from Christ, has messed up the world around them, and almost everything else they have touched. To see that this is true, all you have to do is look around to see what a mess we have made of God's earth. Humans are forever struggling to figure out what went wrong and not willing to admit that their problem is sin and always has been, and refusing, (denial) to admit that Jesus Christ is the only remedy for sin.

It's difficult for humans to admit their denial because when we do that we must also admit that we have been lying to ourselves over the years. Once our denial is grasped, it's necessary for us to admit how powerless we are over our tendency to do the wrong thing. In this step you admit that you are powerless over your addictions and in need of supernatural strength to break free from the chains of those addictions. You've come out of denial, admitted your powerlessness, and now it's time to turn your addiction over to the power of Christ, It takes the power of Christ, through the working of the Holy Spirit, to give you the strength to break the stronghold of nicotine addiction! "I can do all things through Christ who strengthens me" (Phil 4:13).

Many have quit smoking cigarettes, without Christ in their life, and I think that is great, but I wonder how many still long for that addiction? I have been told in recovery circles that once in recovery always in recovery. What that means, to me, is that even though you have quit doing whatever it was you were doing that you still have a desire to do it. I believe that, through the power of the Holy Spirit, you can achieve complete recovery, and totally lose the desire to smoke again.

The complete recovery from nicotine addiction I have experienced, in my own life, is also possible in your life. I believe this can be accomplished through total surrender to Jesus Christ. When you surrender your life to Christ, He gives you a "new heart" and "new desires." I believe that Jesus will complete the process He has begun in you because the Bible tells us He will, "Being confident of this very thing, that He who has begun a good work in you will complete *it* until the day of Jesus Christ" (Phil. 1:6, italics theirs).

If you don't know Christ as savior and Lord, before you read any further, turn not only your addiction, but your life over to Jesus Christ. All have sinned, (cf. Romans 8:23) and in doing so, all, have fallen short of the standards that God set for us when He first created human-beings in the Garden of Eden. We were created in love (cf. John 3:16), and God loves us so much He can't bear the thought of never fellowshipping with us again. So He devised a solution for that problem, and that solution, was to send His only begotten son to earth to die, in our place, on the cross. While Jesus hung dying on that cross, God dumped all the sins of the world on His shoulders; including yours and mine. There's only one thing that God requires for you to be free of sin and that is to accept the free gift of grace, given to all, who, by faith, call on the name of Jesus. A simple prayer can begin this relationship. Lord, I'm sorry for my sins, please forgive me Jesus and be the Lord of my life. Amen! Now that you have done that, and those of you who have done it previously now possess everything you need to quit smoking, chewing, vaping, or whatever it is that's keeping you from being free. Because Christ now lives inside of you, "But if the Spirit of Him who raised Jesus from the dead dwells in you, He who raised Christ from the dead will also give life to your mortal bodies through His Spirit who dwells in you" (Romans 8:11).

You have learned about coming out of denial, you have admitted your powerlessness over your addiction, and you have turned your life and addiction over to Christ. Now it's time to commit to the process of completing the reading and work assignments set forth in this book.

Below you will find a commitment sheet to sign committing to completing the process set forth in this book. Please, read and sign it then put it somewhere where you will be able to read it on a daily basis.

I_____commit to the process of putting-off nicotine addiction, and anything else that hinders me from growing in Christ-likeness. I commit to the process, as described in this program, and taught to us in the Word of God by the apostle Paul from Ephesians 4:22-24. I will trust in Christ and in the power He has given me through the Holy Spirit to put-off this addiction.

I commit to attending every small group session, completing all homework assignments, reading assignments, and memorizing the verses assigned to me. I will build an accountability team and use them throughout this process. By the end of this process, I will have a plan in place to help me sustain a nicotine free life style.

I commit to completely turning this destructive behavior over to Jesus by week four of this process; if not sooner.

Signature_____DATE_____

CHAPTER 3

THE RISK OF SMOKING AND THE BENEFITS OF QUITTING/ NICOTINE WITHDRAWL AND GRAVINGS

Its common knowledge today that cigarette smoke causes pulmonary diseases such as COPD (chronic obstructive pulmonary disease), which includes chronic bronchitis and emphysema. Smoking also increases you chances of getting several forms of cancer. But there's a greater chance, you will die of a heart-related disease than cancer or COPD,

> Although the *relative* risk of cigarette smoking is greater for lung cancer, the *absolute* risk is greatest for coronary diseases and smoking-related coronary deaths amount to some 250,000 yearly compared to 70,000 for cancer.- American Heart Journal (Italics theirs)

As the years of smoking went by, I was diagnosed with high blood pressure which damages the heart and arteries. If high blood pressure wasn't bad enough, I could feel the very Breath, given to me by God, being squeezed from my lungs. I was constantly making trips to the doctor's office for antibiotics. I haven't had a flair-up of bronchitis since I quit smoking. I believe, if I had not quit smoking when I did, I would currently be handcuffed to an oxygen tank or I would be deceased.

It's scary to think about all the good things God has allowed me to experience over the past seventeen years, since I quit smoking. There's so much I could have missed out on. I could have missed being present at the birth of my grandchildren and great grandchildren. I would have squandered an opportunity to become a pastor and missed the privilege to grow even deeper in my relationship with Jesus. Instead of all of that I could be "six feet under."

DISEASES NOT NORMALLY ASSOCIATED WITH CIGARETTE SMOKING

Extensive research conveys the negative effect on the body from smoking:

- Smoking can make it harder for a woman to become pregnant and can affect her baby's health before and after birth.
- Smoking can affect bone health.
- Smoking affects the health of your teeth and gums and can cause tooth loss.
- Smoking can increase your risk for cataracts (clouding of the eye's lens that makes it hard for you to see) and age-related macular degeneration (damage to a small spot near the center of the retina, the part of the eye needed for central vision).
- Smoking is a cause of type 2 diabetes mellitus and can make it harder to control. The risk of developing diabetes is 30–40% higher for active smokers than nonsmokers.

- Smoking causes general adverse effects on the body. It can cause inflammation and adverse effects on immune function.
- Smoking is a cause of rheumatoid arthritis.- A report from the Surgeon General, U.S. Department of Health and Human Services

Some of those diseases really struck home with me: I was diagnosed with type 2 diabetes in 2000, and I have suffered with gum disease and tooth loss over the years. I never connected those two diseases with smoking until now. I hope this information will help you, and will open your eyes to the enormous risks of smoking.

SECOND-HAND SMOKE

Second hand smoke is a real danger. It injures the most innocent of God's children; the very young:

> Worldwide, 40% of children, 33% of male non-smokers, and 35% of female non-smokers were exposed to second-hand smoke in 2004. This exposure was estimated to have caused 379,000 deaths from ischemic heart disease, 165, 000 from lower respiratory infections, 36,900 from asthma, and 21,400 from lung cancer. 603,000 deaths were attributable to second-hand smoke in 2004. - "Worldwide Burden of Disease from Exposure to Second-hand Smoke." The Lancet

THE GOOD NEWS: THE BENEFITS OF QUITTING SMOKING

I have experienced the immediate physical benefits of quitting. In just a couple of days, you begin to breathe better, the coughing continues, but it's cleaning out the buildup of toxins in your lungs and nasal passages and soon the coughing will stop. Your taste for food returns and your sense of smell increases. It's truly amazing how much better you begin to feel; you can actually breathe again! Your body is now getting the proper amount of oxygen instead of processing carbon dioxide.

The Good News: "No matter how old you are or how long you have smoked, quitting can help you live longer and be healthier."– Dr. Lori Brister Deemer M.D.

- Smokers who quit before the age of 50 cut the risk of dying in the next 15 years in half!
- Ex-smokers enjoy a higher quality of life; fewer illnesses like cold, flu, bronchitis, pneumonia; and feel healthier than people who still smoke
- Quitting lowers the risk of many diseases and cancers, lets blood vessels work better, helps heart/lung function
- The younger you quit the more health risks are reduced, but quitting at any age gives back years of life that would be lost while continuing to smoke. - Dr. Lori Brister Deemer M.D.

A study done by the American Journal of Public Health confirms the overwhelming benefits of quitting smoking:

> Our study showed that people live substantially longer when they stop smoking, regardless of the age at which they quit. Most of the excess mortality from smoking could be avoided by quitting smoking at age 35 years, and much of the excess mortality could be avoided by stopping smoking in middle age. These findings reinforce the urgency of emphasizing smoking cessation to all smokers, irrespective of age, and the importance of never assuming that a smoker is "too far gone." Our estimates of the life extension that would accrue from smoking cessation are

conservative. - American Journal of Public Health: Benefits of Smoking Cessation for Longevity.

The American Cancer Society emphasizes the need to quit smoking and confirms that quitting will add years to one's life. "Smokers die significantly earlier than nonsmokers: 13.2 years for men and 14.5 years for women." - American Cancer Society

What delightful experiences could you experience by living 13-14 yrs. longer?

The health benefits of quitting smoking are certainly worth the effort to quit, but there is also a large monetary advantage to quitting smoking. Figuring on smoking one pack a day at the current price of a brand name of cigarettes (I was a two pack a day smoker so you could double the cost in my case). Yearly cost of smoking: 1 pack a day, ($5.74) X 365 = $2,095.10, in Ten Years: 2,095.10 X 10 (Next ten years) = $20,951.00. – The economic cost of smoking and benefits of quitting for individual smokers.

What could you do with an extra $2,000.00- $4000.00 a year? Make a list.

There are also spiritual rewards for quitting. For instance, quitting will add power to your witness for Christ. A personal witness to the power of Christ that enables you to overcome such a powerful chemical addiction is powerful.

NICOTINE WITHDRAWL AND CRAVINGS

Nicotine is an addictive substance, and once you stop feeding your brains addiction to it your body is going to react in a rebellious way. Nicotine withdrawal is not a life-threatening condition. It takes 3-4 days for nicotine to completely leave your body. That is the period when nicotine withdrawal will be at its peak. In most cases the symptoms, generally, go away after two weeks, but can hang on for several months.

Below is a list of nicotine withdrawal symptoms to be on the lookout for:

- Sadness or depression.
- Irritability and anger.
- Difficulty concentrating, restlessness, and insomnia.
- Decreased heart rate.
- Increased appetite.

Along with the symptoms of nicotine withdrawal, you will likely experience strong cravings for a cigarette. The good news is that cravings only last for a few moments. If you can resist for those few minutes the craving will go away. Cravings normally will decrease in intensity and frequency in a week or two and should completely come to an end in 1-3 months.

The great news is that the biblical principles set forth in this process, to help you kick the cigarette habit, will help you overcome nicotine withdrawal and cravings. When those symptoms occur, you immediately replace them with something else (cf. chapter five). Replace them with prayer, read your Bible, do something with your hands, exercise, etc. Put on something positive to get your mind off the withdrawal symptoms or cravings.

Chapter 4

MY PERSONAL BATTLE TO QUIT SMOKING

I have often felt powerless over situations in my life, and being drafted in 1970 was one of those times. Short of going to jail, there was nothing I could do about the selective service process. That was a situation in my life where I had no choice but to do what my country had called me to do.

Alcohol was an addictive habit that I chose to do and I soon felt powerless to overcome that addiction. The fear of living my life without alcohol was crippling to me especially after using alcohol, as a crutch, for so many years. I wondered how I could cope with life's problems sober. In reality, I created problems by drinking? Finally, after many years of brokenness, shame, guilt, and when I could no longer stand the pain any longer, I was forced to come out of denial and admit that I either had to quit drinking or I was going to die. After giving my life to Christ on February 13, 2000, I was able to put-off alcohol addiction. I haven't drunk an alcoholic beverage since that day. What a miracle!

I had been a Christian for about six months when God convicted me about smoking. I was telling others how Jesus could set them free from their addictions and help them put their lives back together. But, evidently, God couldn't deliver me from cigarettes. It was so frustrating! I can't recall what led up to this special night, but I finally got so fed up with feeling helpless I set down on an old, worn out, dingy colored couch in my living room. After sitting a while, I finally admitted to myself and to God that smoking was harmful for me, harmful to those around me, and not pleasing to the Lord (step one: coming out of denial).

I will never forget that night. I had about a half of a pack of cigarettes left, so I sat down on the couch and smoked one cigarette after another until I was down to the very last one. As I took those last few deadly drags from that cigarette and right before I put that last cigarette out I said a little prayer. I still remember today clearly saying, "Jesus, I know I can't do this on my own (admitting powerlessness) it's in your hands now" (turning it over to Christ). The simplest prayers can make the biggest difference. I put that last cigarette out on July 3, 2000, and I haven't smoked a cigarette since.

I didn't understand, then, that the Lord had taken me through a process in the months leading up to that night as the steps to recovery, until I got involved in a Celebrate Recovery ministry. While learning about recovery, I realized the process that the Lord had taken me through was the same as the first three steps of recovery: admitting your denial, admitting your powerlessness, and turning your addiction over to Jesus.

No matter how powerless you feel over this addiction, we serve a God that is willing and able to give you the strength to overcome your addiction. I assure you that the God who on the first day of creation said, "Let there be light and there was light" wants to see you set free from this addiction so you can better serve Him. A couple of the Scriptures that helped me in this battle to be smoke free are Philippians 4:13, "I can do all things through Christ who strengthens me," and Romans 8:28, "And we know that all things work together for good to those who love God, to those who are called according to His purpose." I certainly don't intend to imply that quitting smoking is going to be easy because it's not. However, I can testify to you that through the power of Christ it can be done; I'm undeniable proof of that.

INTRODUCTION TO THE PROCESS

The process outlined in this book is based on counseling techniques, recovery principles and fueled by the power of the Scriptures. In these coming chapters, we are going to work hard and trust in the power of the Holy Spirit to give us the strength to be victorious. The tools we are going to use are based on biblical principles according to the Apostle Paul's teaching from Ephesians 4:22-24.

THIS PROCESS CONSISTS OF THE FOLLOWING REQUIREMENTS

1. Completing Bible reading assignments.
2. Completing homework assignments based on the reading assignments?
3. There will be regular prayer and Scripture memorization.
4. You will build an accountability team.
5. You will learn the importance of living a healthier life style.

The materials you will need to work through this process are this book, a pen, a notebook, a Bible, and some 3x5 cards. Let's get started!

Chapter 5

EPHESIANS 4:22-24: PUT-OFFS/ PUT-ONS/UNFORGIVENESS/ SETTING GOALS

WEEK ONE PROCESS AND READING ASSIGNMENTS

Using your note pad and pen begin a put-off list. Put-offs are the triggers that cause you to want to smoke. Examples: I always smoke after eating, or I always light up when I drive. As you identify these triggers and begin to put-off those bad habits you will identify and put-on new Christ honoring habits to take their place. This process is based on sound biblical instruction from Ephesians 4:22-24. (The process of putting on Christ (cf. Romans 8:29)

I want to emphasize the importance of being diligent as you identify the put-offs associated with smoking. The put-offs and put-ons is the doctrine of how a Christians changes, and can be applied the rest of your life to overcome the undesirable traits you struggle with, and how to replace them with Christ-honoring traits.

During my years serving as a biblical counselor and in a recovery ministry, I counseled and mentored several struggling Christians. I observed that those who worked hard in their walk with Christ were successful in overcoming the sinful behavior that kept them bound. On the other hand, those who set around waiting for something to change in their lives, without putting in the effort necessary to grow in Christ-likeness continuously struggled, and soon returned to "wallowing in the mud," as the Scriptures warn us might happen.

Don't let the enemy deceive you! It's crucial, if you are going to grow in Christ-likeness that you do the work necessary to grow. Do you want a "status quo" Christian life, or do you want a life filled with joy, love, peace, and freedom from addiction? Creating a vibrant Christian walk requires time, effort, and commitment. Be a student of the Bible, develop a strong prayer life, and surround yourself with godly men/woman who teach and encourage you and give freely of yourself to others. If you are unwilling to do the necessary work, it will be very difficult to change your situation and realize the freedoms you have been given in Christ. The great news is that as you develop this Christ-like character the things that bind you will begin to fall off of you like melting snow falling off a hot roof.

Read Ephesians 4:22-24 and answer the question below. Be prepared to discuss the question next week in small group. If you are doing this on your own, find a trusted Christian non-smoker to walk through this process and discuss these questions with them.

1. According to these Scriptures, what do you see as the key to putting-off old destructive habits and putting-on new Christ honoring habits?

2. Write a prayer, in your own words, asking Jesus to give you the strength to quit smoking and to give you the faith to believe that through Christ you can do this. Pray this prayer throughout this process.

MEMORIZATION SCRIPTURES

"I can do all things through Christ who strengthens me" (Philippians 4:13).

"May the God of hope fill you with all joy and peace in believing, that you may abound in hope by the power of the Holy Spirit" (Romans 15:13).

Use 3x5 cards to write down memorization Scriptures and carry them with you, put them on your sun visor, or even on your cell phone. This is the process of putting-off unwholesome thoughts and replacing them with the Word of God: "working the power of Scriptures."

INDIVIDUAL/SMALL GROUP QUESTIONS TO ANSWER THIS WEEK

1. What situations trigger your desire to light-up?

2. How is smoking benefiting you or those around you?

3. List the excuses you have used in the past to deny the need to quit smoking?

Be prepared to discuss your answers with your small group/trusted friend. These questions are designed to help you come out of denial, admit your powerlessness, and turn your smoking addiction over to Christ.

LESSON ONE

This week's teaching is on Ephesians 4:22-24 putting-off the old man and putting-on the new man. Verse twenty-three instructs us to do that by the renewing of our mind. That sounds simple enough, but how do you renew your mind? Are there "mind renewing garages" where we can take our minds in to be changed every five years? Is there a place where we can get a brain tune-up every ten years to wipe away the negative thoughts we accumulate? I wish it was that easy, but in reality, it takes hard work to put-off those old habits and to keep them off. We must replace the defeating thoughts and actions that want to dominate our thoughts and put-on Christ honoring thoughts and habits, allowing Christ to dominate our thoughts.

Proverbs 23:7 says, "For as he thinks in his heart so is he." The battle for our souls and freedom from addictions is fought in the mind. The mind creates thoughts, and those thoughts are communicated to the heart and from the heart proceeds actions. Changing the way we think about smoking will directly affect our power to quit; as we come out of denial, admit our powerlessness over our addiction, and turning this addictive behavior over to Christ. Believing we can quit, through the power of Jesus, will change our thought process by communicating new information to the heart resulting in a change of personal habits and desires.

The heart motivates the bodies' actions. Scripture teaches us that in proverbs, "Above all else, guard your heart, for everything you do flows from it" (Prov. 4:23 NIV). Not only must we guard our hearts, not allowing bad things to get in there, there are times when we need to re-program our minds: changing our thinking from addictive thinking to non-addictive thinking. After making this change, we will no longer define our identity as a smoker, but we will identify ourselves as children of God and non-smokers. That in a "nut-shell" is the putting-off and putting-on process from Ephesians 4:22-24. This process will change our focus from addiction to non-addiction helping us find freedom in Jesus Christ.

After committing my Life to Christ I needed to live a more disciplined life. I had to change the way I think and establish new priorities in my life: putting-off the old way of thinking and putting-on a new way of thinking. There were four biblical disciplines that were crucial in helping me in the process of renewing my mind. The most significant biblical discipline for Christians to practice in order to grow in their Christian walk and renew the mind is to read and meditate on the Bible every day. Memorizing God's Word is made clear in the Scriptures, "Therefore you shall lay up these words of mine in your heart and in your soul, and bind them as a sign upon your hand, and they shall be as frontlets between your eyes" (Deuteronomy 11:18). Colossians 3:16 tells us to, "…Let the word of Christ dwell in you richly." Dwell, in this verse, means to let the Word of God actively live inside of your heart: "working the power of the Scriptures, changing the focus of the heart." let God's Word become a living part of your very fiber that inner being, called the soul. The only way to do that is to read, memorize, and study God's Word daily. Hebrews 4:12 reminds us of the power of God's Word "… it is alive and powerful." The power that exists, in the Word of God, is the conquering power we need to defeat this giant of nicotine addiction once and for all.

Reading and meditating on the Scriptures daily refreshes you, renews the mind, and gives you hope and peace. It's essential for you to become a student of the Bible in order to change the way you think. Take a moment right now and think about how much time you spend on a daily basis in God's Word and where you can find more time, in your busy day, to study God's Word.

To get in the habit of reading God's word every day, begin by setting a time and place to read the Bible and stick to it. Where do I begin reading in the Bible? Here are a few things I have done in the past to get started (getting started can be the hardest part). Begin by reading the Psalms. There are one hundred and fifty Psalms and that takes a while to get through. After reading through the Psalms read through the Book of Proverbs. You could start by reading through the gospels: Matthew, Mark, Luke, and John and continue on through the epistles. The important thing is to get started and once you do, you will look forward to spending time in God's Word. Hopefully, after a while, you will develop an addiction to spending time with the Lord and His Word each day. That is an addiction that is well-pleasing to the Lord Jesus and rewarding to you.

The second biblical discipline we need to develop is to pray continuously. Prayer, in its simplest form, is simply talking to God one-on-one. We pray because we are putting our trust in God and depending on His power to give us the strength to stop smoking. Do you trust God with your prayers? Do you make time alone in prayer with God a priority? Your prayer life will only be as important as you make it. Prayer is your personal conversation with the creator of the whole universe. Take advantage of that divine connection. The apostle Paul wrote, "Pray without ceasing" (1 Thessalonians 5:17).

Paul in that short verse makes a profound statement regarding the importance of prayer in building a relationship with Jesus. You can't build relationships without communicating with one another and spending time together. Take a moment here and think about how much time you spend alone talking to Jesus and where, during your busy day, can you find more time to spend in prayer. The good thing about prayer is that you can do it anytime and anywhere you want: pray while driving, pray when cleaning, pray while you are going for a walk; get in the habit of praying continuously.

The third biblical discipline we need to cultivate is to fellowship with other believers. Fellowship with other Christians will help in building an accountability team as you go through this process. The biblical discipline of gathering together is also grounded in Scripture, "Not forsaking the assembling of ourselves together, as is the manner of some, but exhorting one another: and so much the more, as you see the Day approaching" (Hebrews 10:25).

The Christian life was never meant to be lived in isolation. We need each other to encourage and edify one another especially during the tough times. There are going to be tough times as we grow in our daily walk with Jesus. Take a moment and think about how often you meet with other Christians. Once a week on Sunday mornings is good, but it's not enough. You should have at least two or more fellowship events each week. You can increase your Christian fellowship by joining a small group, a bible study, or a prayer team. After your victory over nicotine addiction, you could start a Christian support group for those who have quit smoking. That would be a fellowship event.

The fourth biblical discipline we need to develop is serving. Serving in ministry with other believers is crucial for building healthy relationships and creating an accountability team. The servant's heart was modeled by Christ when He was here on this earth. It was important enough to Jesus that one of the last things He taught His disciples, before He went to the cross, was the importance of serving, "If I then, your Lord and Teacher, have washed your feet, you also ought to wash one another's feet. For I have given you an example, that you should do as I have done to you" (John 13:14-15). Jesus said in the Gospel of Mark, "For even the Son of Man did not come to be served, but to serve, and to give His life a ransom for many" (Mark 10:45).

We are never more like Christ then when we are giving of ourselves to others.

Serving others in a ministry is a great way to build Christ honoring, healthy relationships. In some cases, while in recovery, it may be necessary to sever some destructive relationships. This will allow you to begin making new healthy relationships. In cases that involve family members or coworkers severing a relationship may not be possible, but make it clear to those family members or coworkers that you are committed to quitting smoking, and insist on their help and support. Gaining the support of those close to you such as friends and family is important not only for quitting now, but for sustaining a smoke free life style.

If you are not serving in a Christian ministry, or don't know where to serve ask other Christians where they serve. Join a ministry that feeds the homeless; be a greeter at church. There is a great need for people to serve in the Body of Christ. Take a moment and list the Christian ministries you are active in; if there aren't any, make a list of Christian ministries that interest you and begin serving in them (take action).

It's through the practicing of these biblical disciplines that we will accomplish the process of renewing our minds, with the goal of developing Christ-like character. Review the four biblical disciplines listed in this chapter and evaluate where you stand on each one:

1. Read and study the Bible daily.
2. Pray without ceasing.
3. Fellowship with other believers.
4. Serve in a Church ministry.

There are several other biblical disciplines you can develop as you grow in your Christian walk, but these four will give you a strong foundation to build on.

Living a more disciplined life was a crucial part in helping me grow early on in my new found faith. In addition to my lack of discipline, I struggled with anger and unforgiveness towards those who had hurt me in the past. It didn't take Jesus long to reveal to me the necessity to forgive all those old wounds. Jesus said, during the Sermon on the Mount, that if we don't forgive others their trespasses, against us; God won't forgive our trespasses against Him (cf. Matthew 6:15).

We must never forget that smoking cigarettes is an addiction to nicotine. While counseling others, with addictions, I found that one of the keys to recovery is dealing with your own anger and forgiving those who have hurt you in the past. In many cases, the ones you are refusing to forgive are not even aware they have offended you, or they could care less if they have. Unforgiveness could be described as shooting yourself in the foot and expecting the other person to be hopping around. Unforgiveness only hurts you and those you love. Anger and stress are key triggers in wanting to light-up and unforgiveness is a cause of stress and anger.

Forgiving others is a painful yet a crucial part of your recovery process and the renewing of your mind: replacing angry, hurtful thoughts with thoughts of love, joy, peace, and forgiveness. One of the things I did to help me forgive those who hurt me was to pray for the person that I felt wronged me, and eventually I was able to forgive them. The forgiveness of those who have hurt you deeply doesn't happen overnight, so remain persistent in your prayers for them. Oh what wonderful freedom comes from those three little words, "I forgive you!"

No one is asking you to spend time with the person who has hurt you. In cases of sexual and physical abuse, it might not be advisable. Although, I do believe, through the power of Jesus Christ that complete healing and reconciliation can happen. Only the one who has been abused can decide to reconcile with the abuser. I've known family members who haven't spoken to one another for years over some forgotten event. That's a shame for them and other family members. Forgiving others is not an option it's commanded for us to do by Jesus (cf. Matthew 6: 14, 15). Regardless of the depth of the pain you have experienced, it's critical to forgive those who have hurt you.

I know thinking about forgiving others can be a daunting task, but take a few moments and make a confidential list of those you need to forgive, and begin seeking Jesus' help and for the strength to forgive them. Remember that Christ has forgiven you. Forgiving others is truly a necessary step on the road to recovery; and essential to find the joy and peace that comes from a right relationship with Jesus.

SETTING GOALS

In order to help us live a more disciplined life, we need to set goals. God set goals for Himself. From the fall of humankind, God set a goal to reconcile fallen humanity to Himself through His son Jesus, "In this is love, not that we loved God, but that He loved us and sent His Son *to be* the propitiation (substitute) for our sins" (1 John 4:10 italics theirs, emphasis mine).

Satan also has specific goals he wants to accomplish. Jesus said this about Satan, "The thief does not come except to steal, and to kill, and to destroy..." (John 10:10). Satan's goal is to achieve the destruction of lives. That's what smoking is doing to those who smoke, and sometimes to those who don't. Smoking cigarettes destroys your joy, your witness to others for Christ; it steals your money and gives it to large corporate tobacco companies bent on getting folks addicted to nicotine which in many cases kills them. So ask yourself, why do you continue to smoke cigarettes? The purchasing of tobacco products enables the tobacco companies to continue to market those harmful products.

Jesus set goals for His church. He said, "All authority has been given to Me in heaven and on earth. Go therefore and make disciples of all the nations, baptizing them in the name of the Father and of the Son and of the Holy Spirit, teaching them to observe all things that I have commanded you; and lo, I am with you always, even to the end of the age" (Matthew 28:18-20). Jesus, right before He ascended into heaven, gave the church a goal to evangelize the whole world.

God also set a personal goal for His children, "For whom He foreknew, He also predestined to be conformed to the image of His Son, that He might be the firstborn among many brethren" (Romans 8:29). God set a goal for us to be conformed to the image of His son Jesus. We can't completely accomplish that goal if we are in bondage to nicotine or anything else? Do you set personal goals when it comes to your daily, weekly, monthly, yearly, and beyond in your Christian walk? What are some things you should be setting goals for?

1. The time you spend alone with the Lord.
    a. Time spent studying the bible.

      b. Time spent in prayer.
2. Time spent in fellowship with other believers.
3. Time spent serving.

How often do you sit down and read the Bible and meditate on it? How much time do you spend alone in prayer with God with no distractions? No distractions mean: no phone calls or texts, no computer, no radio and T.V., just one-on-one with the Lord. How many times a week do you spend fellowshipping with other believers? Are you giving back by serving others? Examining ourselves helps us to evaluate our strengths and weaknesses so that we can build on our weaknesses, while maintaining our strengths. "Let us search out and examine our ways, and turn back to the Lord" (Lamentations 3:40). It's scriptural to examine our lives and evaluate our relationship with Christ while taking time to study the progress we are making on the path to Christ-likeness. If we don't examine the path we've been on, how can we make corrections and see clearly in what direction we should go?

It's only through practicing biblical disciplines that we are able to renew our minds: putting-off the old man and putting-on Christ-likeness. The renewing of the mind frees us of the things that keep us in bondage. It's not easy to break the chains of addiction or forgive those who have hurt us. It takes hard work and self-discipline in partnership with the Holy Spirit, but it can be done. Set some goals this week in those four biblical disciplines, grant forgiveness to those who have hurt you. Stick to it and see how quickly God begins to renew your mind.

CHAPTER 6

TRUSTING IN GOD'S STRENGTH
1 SAMUEL 17:1-51

WEEK TWO PROCESS AND READING ASSIGNMENTS

Continue compiling your put-off list! Be diligent compiling this list!

Read the story of David and Goliath 1 Samuel 17:1-51.

Answer each of these questions and be prepared to discuss them in small group next week.

1. Whose strength was David depending on to defeat Goliath?

2. How can you use the biblical truths in this story to conquer the giant of nicotine addiction in your life?

3. Do you consider nicotine addiction an idol (biblical definition of an idol "a worthless thing" (cf. 1 Chronicles 16:26)?

MEMORIZATIION SCRIPTURES

"Do you not know that your body is a temple of the Holy Spirit, who is in you, whom you have from God, and you are not your own; for you were bought at a price. Therefore glorify God in your body and in your spirit, which are God's (1 Corinthians 6:19-20).

"...The Lord does not save with sword and spear; for the battle is the Lord's..." (1 Samuel 17: 47).

INDIVIDUAL/SMALL GROUP QUESTIONS TO ANSWER THIS WEEK

1. By smoking, how are you harming your body?

2. By smoking, how are you harming others?

3. How often have you tried to quit smoking and failed? Explain. Answer the question why did I fail?

LESSON TWO

Obedience to God's call was a trait that David possessed which drew him to the battle ground and the victory over Goliath. In order for you to defeat the giant of nicotine addiction you will need to be obedient to your "Father in Heaven."

David obeyed his father, Jesse, when he instructed him to go to the battle where David's brothers were, "So David rose early in the morning, left the sheep with a keeper, and took the things and went as Jesse had commanded him. And he came to the camp as the army was going out to the fight and shouting for the battle" (1 Sam. 17:20).

What are some actions you could take to enable you to be obedient to Christ's commands? Remember the teaching last week when we learned about the four biblical disciplines: reading the Bible, prayer, fellowship with other Believers, and serving others. These are action steps that will help you to understand God's call on your life, and strengthen you in being obedient to that call.

Stop here for a few moments and list some other actions you can take that will empower you to be obedient to Jesus' call on your life.

David understood it was God calling him to the battle, and being obedient to God's call he went. That faint whisper you have been hearing in your ear for a while now, "it's time to quit," is God calling you to victory over nicotine addiction. In defeating this giant of nicotine addiction, you need to be obedient to God's call to go to the battle. Remember that you are not at this point in your life by accident. God brought you here. God has sent you to this battle and He will be with you throughout this process. Jesus promised that He would never leave us alone nor forsake us (cf. Hebrews 13:5).

DO NOT ALLOW PEOPLE OR CIRCUMSTANCES TO DISCOURAGE YOU

David didn't allow those around him to discourage him from doing what he knew God had called him to do, "And Saul said to David, you are not able to go against this Philistine to fight with him; for you *are* a youth, and he a man of war from his youth" (1Sam. 17:33 italics theirs).

There are those around you, in ways they may not even realize, that are going to discourage you. You must not let that happen! Stay focused on Jesus and the battle ahead. Saul, the King of Israel, a person of great authority in David's life was telling David that he was nothing but a child and it would be impossible for him to have the victory over such a large warrior.

In spite of that discouragement, David stayed obedient to God's call. He refused to listen to earthly authority; instead, he trusted in heavenly authority. You must not listen to those around you who try to discourage you. Transcribe these words on your heart, "The battle belongs to the Lord." Don't allow those around you to discourage you and don't allow the obstacles that are sure to come your way discourage you. You are in a battle for your life just like David.

RECALL VICTORIES FROM THE PAST TO ENCOURAGE OURSELVES IN THE LORD

David recalled the times in the past where the Lord had delivered him from what seemed like insurmountable odds such as battling with a lion and a bear while tending his father's sheep

1 Sam. 17:34-36,

> But David said to Saul, "Your servant used to keep his father's sheep, and when a lion or a bear came and took a lamb out of the flock, I went out after it and struck it, and delivered the lamb from its mouth; and when it arose against me, I caught it by its beard, and struck and killed it. Your servant has killed both lion and bear; and this uncircumcised Philistine will be like one of them, seeing he has defied the armies of the living God.

Its "life-giving" to remember the times that the Lord reached down from heaven, rescued you, fought for you, and delivered you from harm. You should never forget God's faithfulness, or how much He loves you and how he has fought for you in the past.

Take a few moments and recall the times the Lord was present strengthening you. Always keep in mind His death on the cross of Calvary. He gave His life for you!

PUT ON THE WHOLE ARMOR OF GOD AND PREPARE YOURSELF FOR THE BATTLE

David, in preparation for the battle, knew what his weapons were and he knew how and when to use them. Don't go into a spiritual battle without putting on the "Whole Armor of God" (cf. chapter nine) putting no faith in the weapons of this world, "David fastened his sword to his armor and tried to walk, for he had not tested them. And David said to Saul, "I cannot walk with these, for I have not tested them." So David took them off" (1 Sam. 17:39).

It must have been a comical scene to see David put on man-made armor while preparing to face the giant. I wonder what God thought as He watched the man after His own heart weigh himself down with earthly armor; I imagine He smiled. In the fight to be nicotine free, remember that your battle is a spiritual battle not an earthly one. Anytime you do something for the Lord there will be a spiritual battle to fight.

The Man-made armor David put on was so heavy it weighed him down to the point where he couldn't walk; let alone fight. David understood that it was God's armor he needed. Cast off man-made weapons and put on God-made weapons: trust in Christ, the truth of the Scriptures, love, joy, peace, faith, perseverance, prayer, obedience, humility, etc., "Then he took his staff in his hand; and he chose for himself five smooth stones from the brook, and put them in a shepherd's bag, in a pouch which he had, and his sling was in his hand. And he drew near to the Philistine" (1 Sam. 17:40).

The most powerful weapons in a spiritual battle are not dynamite but five smooth stones called, the Word of God, faith, prayer, trust, and obedience to God's call.

JIM MORELAND

DO NOT LISTEN TO THE THREATS AND LIES OF THE ENEMY

David didn't listen to the threats and lies of his enemy, "So the Philistine said to David, 'Am I a dog that you come to me with sticks?' And the Philistine cursed David by his gods. And the Philistine said to David, 'Come to me, and I will give your flesh to the birds of the air and the beasts of the field!' (1 Sam. 17:43-44).

Who can we compare Goliath to in these verses? We can compare him to the devil: spitting out threats and lies, mocking and making fun of us, and accusing us before the Father. Satan has no power over God's children, "My Father, who has given *them* to Me, is greater than all; and no one is able to snatch *them* out of My Father's hand" (John 10:29 italics theirs). What if David would have believed those threats and lies from the enemy and gave up. Would he have had known the sweet taste of victory over Goliath, and the freedom that came from his victory?

Don't be tricked into believing a lie; be strong in the Lord and in the power of His might. The devil's greatest tool is to create doubt in the minds of God's children about the goodness of the Lord. Satan has no new weapons in his arsenal. In the Garden of Eden he created doubt in the mind of Eve. Then tempted her with the same temptations he still uses today: the lust of the flesh, Eve, "wouldn't that fruit be good for food?" The lusts of the eyes, Eve, "look how pretty that fruit is." The pride of life, Eve, "if you eat that fruit you will be like God" (cf. Gen. 3:1-7).

The devil used the same tricks on Jesus in the wilderness: "If you be the son of God (doubt) turn these stones into bread (flesh)." "If you are the son of God (doubt) throw yourself off of this temple" "for it is written, the angels of God will come and save you" (Pride). The devils final temptation, offered to Jesus: "Look at all the world down there Jesus it will all be yours if you bow down and worship me" (lust of the eyes) (cf. Matt. 4:1-10). Same old lies! Don't fall for those same old tricks. Fight back with the

Scriptures, like Jesus did. Trust in the truths you have learned from reading the Bible.

Be diligent and be on the lookout for those same tricks. They may come in different forms, but at their root, they are still the same old, worn out lies Satan has always used to create doubt in your mind; "Did God say." When the "Lord of Lords" and "King of Kings" was confronted by Satan in the wilderness He used the same weapon to repel the attacks of Satan that is still available to us today: "The Word of God." The Word of God has not changed, nor has its power been diminished. The lesson learned from these verses is that if Jesus used "The Word of God" in His battle against the wiles of the devil, how much more should we use the Scriptures in our battle? Work the power of the Scriptures in every battle you face and in every minute of the day and night. A spiritual weapon is not a weapon if you don't use it.

THE BATTLE BELONGS TO THE LORD

David understood that the Lord was going to deliver Goliath into his hand. Remember that God's will is for you to be free of this addiction, and He will fight for you, if you will let Him. David trusted in God's power, not his own, 1 Sam 17:45-47,

> Then David said to the Philistine, "You come to me with a sword, with a spear, and with a javelin. But I come to you in the name of the LORD of hosts, the God of the armies of Israel, whom you have defied. This day the LORD will deliver you into my hand, and I will strike you and take your head from you. And this day I will give the carcasses of the camp of the Philistines to the birds of the air and the wild beasts of the earth, that all the earth may know that there is a God in Israel. Then

> all this assembly shall know that the LORD does not save with sword and spear; for the battle *is* the LORD's, and He will give you into our hands (italics theirs).

David understood that this was the Lord's battle to fight, not his. God's desire is to deliver you from smoking and anything else that hinderers your walk with Him. When we surrender wholly to the Lord: trusting in the Holy Spirit to lead us into battle and taking full advantage of the spiritual weapons available to us; we will be victorious. The problem arises when we try to do things on our own strength instead of depending on God's strength to get us through. When that happens, we usually end up discouraged, defeated, and worse off than we were before.

Scripture instructs us to come boldly into the throne of grace: into the very presence of God. We can be bold in our battle against this giant of nicotine addiction because the victory has already been won for us by Jesus. All we have to do is reach out and take it. I love the boldness of David's heart, as he confronted Goliath in 1 Samuel 17:45, "You come to me with sword and spear, and with a javelin. But I come to you in the name of the Lord of Hosts, the God of the armies of Israel whom you have defied."

You are in a spiritual battle; don't try to fight this battle with earthly weapons. Remember how David got weighed down trying to use man's armor, "For the weapons of our warfare are not carnal but mighty in God for pulling down strongholds" (2 Corinthians 10:4).

What are the giants in our lives but strongholds that keep us bound? These strongholds give Satan a foothold in our lives. When you are struggling with temptations, "work the power available to you in the Scriptures" to give you strength, stop and pray, and use the spiritual weapons God has given you to find victory in this battle: God's Word, faith, hope, love, perseverance, and prayer. The battle is the Lord's, so call upon Him and He will go before you to the battle.

Chapter 7

ACCOUNTABILITY TEAMS
ECCLESIASTICS 4:9-12

WEEK THREE PROCESS AND READING ASSIGNMENTS:

Continue compiling your put-off list! Be diligent compiling this list!

Read Ecclesiastes 4:9-12 and answer this question.

1. According to these Scriptures, why is an accountability team important in helping you quit smoking?

MEMORIZATION SCRIPTURES

"While they promise them freedom, they themselves are slaves of corruption; for by whom a person is overcome, by him also he is brought into bondage" (2 Peter 2:19).

"…but God is faithful; who will not let you be tempted beyond what you are able. But with the temptation will also make the way of escape that you may be able to bear it" (1 Corinthians 10:13).

INDIVIDUAL/SMALL GROUP QUESTIONS TO ANSWER THIS WEEK

1. By quitting smoking, how are you benefiting your physical and spiritual health?

2. How much money do you spend on cigarettes in a year? Include doctor visits and medications for smoking related health issues.

3. What positive things could you do with the extra money you save by not purchasing cigarettes? (Make a list, be specific).

LESSON THREE

From the very beginning of creation, God knitted two people together to strengthen them for the tasks He assigned them to do, "...It is not good for man to be alone; I will make him a helper comparable to him" (Genesis 2:18). We know that God created Eve to be a wife for Adam, but the principle in this verse is to provide a help mate for Adam: someone to come alongside of him and help. Two are stronger than one. Giving them a better chance of accomplishing the task set before them.

Even though Christ is sufficient to meet our needs, God chose to provide Adam with a help mate. God's original plan was to fellowship with Adam and Eve in the garden, but sin got in the way, "And they heard the sound of the LORD God walking in the garden in the cool of the day, and Adam and his wife hid themselves from the presence of the LORD God among the trees of the garden" (Genesis 3:8).

This Scripture teaches that God descended from heaven seeking fellowship with Adam and Eve. When you get alone with God, do you feel Him walking with you in your garden? The garden is a place where we can experience God's presence walking with us through the many trials and tribulations in life. The garden God seeks to walk in is your heart. God above all else wants your heart to belong to Him. Even with God's presence in the garden Adam and Eve failed. Why? They made the mistake of believing a lie instead of the truth of God's Word. Who are you going to believe? Are you going to believe, "I can do all things through Christ who strengthens me," "With God all things are possible," "There's victory in Jesus," or are you going to believe Satan's lies, "You can't do this," "You are going to fail," "Smoking's not so bad," "You aren't hurting anyone else." Jesus warned us that Satan is the father of lies, and is unable to tell the truth (cf. John 8:44) so don't believe anything he says.

Take a moment to write down some of the lies the enemy has been filling your head with, and beside those lies write down the truths found in God's Word.

Jesus confirmed in the New Testament the biblical principle that two are better than one, "And He called the twelve to Himself, and began to send them out two by two, and gave them power over unclean spirits. He commanded them to take nothing for the journey except a staff—no bag, no bread, no copper in their money belts— but to wear sandals, and not to put on two tunics" (Mark 6:7-9).

Why did Jesus tell His disciples not to take anything with them? I think it was because He wanted His disciples to trust in Him to supply all their needs, both materially and spiritually, just like He wants us to trust in Him for the essentials of life. Jesus understood the importance of Solomon's wisdom that two together are better than one. So Jesus sent His disciples out two-by-two, in ministry teams, to minister to the people.

Another story in the New Testament where Jesus confirms this biblical truth is found in the Gospel of Matthew, "Again I say to you that if two of you agree on earth concerning anything that they ask, it will be done for them by My Father in heaven. For where two or three are gathered together in My name, I am there in the midst of them" (Matt. 18:19-20).

It's powerful when two or three of God's children gather together in the name of Christ and pray because Jesus promises to be right there in the heart of it. Jesus said, "I am there," it's not a question of will He be there; but a promise, "I will be there in the midst of them." If you are in a small group right now gather together and pray in agreement for one another to overcome this giant of nicotine addiction. If you are going through this process alone remember that doesn't mean you are alone. Christ is with you! Get down on your knees and pray for Christ to give you the strength to defeat this giant of nicotine addiction.

Putting our faith in the word of God and His power, not our own, will bring victory over this giant of nicotine addiction that is preventing you from being all that God has created you to be. Christ is in the midst of your addiction. You are not in this alone. Show you trust in Jesus by turning your nicotine addiction over to Him right now.

CHAPTER 8

GOD'S LOVE MATTHEW 11:28-30

WEEK FOUR PROCESS AND READING ASSIGNMENTS

Continue compiling your put off list! Be diligent in compiling this list!

Your reading exercise this week was to read Matt. 11:28-30. After reading these verses, answer this question, what five promises does Jesus make to His children in these verses? Make your own list and then compare your list to the list below.

The Five promises:
1. Jesus promises if you come to Him He will not turn you away.
2. Jesus promises to give your soul rest.
3. He promises to teach you.
4. He promises to be yoked together with you.
5. Jesus promises to be gentle with you.

MEMORIZATION SCRIPTURES

"Commit your way to the Lord, trust also in Him and He shall bring it to pass" (Psalm 37:5).

"In all your ways acknowledge Him and He shall direct your paths" (Proverbs 3:6).

INDIVIDUA SMALL/GROUP QUESTIONS TO ANSWER THIS WEEK

1. What strongholds have been keeping you from turning your nicotine addiction over to God?

2. What's your biggest fear when you think about quitting smoking?

3. Do you think God wants you to smoke? If not, why not? Do you believe that God can set you free from nicotine addiction?

LESSON FOUR

Let's examine these verses from Matthew. Jesus said, "Come to me those of you who are burdened." What are you burdened with, fear of failure, fear of being rejected by others, fear of surviving without cigarettes; all the above? Jesus is pleading with you to unload those heavy burdens on Him regardless of what those burdens might be guilt, shame, worry, doubt, unforgiveness, or an addiction. Whatever burdens you are carrying Jesus is pleading with you too cast those burdens upon Him. Be obedient to God's call and heave those burdens in the direction of the cross of Christ. Take a few minutes, right now, and list your burdens (on a separate piece of paper) then ceremoniously cast them off. Then tear that list into pieces and throw those burdens in the trash where they belong.

Secondly, Jesus said, "To take His yoke upon you and learn of me (Yoke meaning to be bonded together with Him) for I am gentle and lowly in heart." Jesus is calling out to you to be like Him: be gentle, be kind, and be humble: put-on Christ-like character traits (spiritual formation)." Being yoked together with Christ, will bring rest for your soul. If only, we would listen, and do what Jesus instructs us to do what glorious victories we could experience.

Too often we think we can do things on our own efforts. Believing we don't need the Lord. When we try accomplishing life-changing circumstances on our own it usually doesn't turn out well. Everything we do should be for one reason and that reason is to please the Lord, "Therefore, whether you eat or drink, or whatever you do, do all to the glory of God" (1 Corinthians 10:31).

Finally, Jesus says in verse 30, "For my yoke is easy and my burden is light." In order to lighten our burdens, we are to join ourselves to Jesus, which allows the Lord to carry those burdens for us. We have access to His strength. All we have to do is grab a hold of it. We no longer have to tackle this addiction on our own. We have the power of Christ living inside of us through the indwelling of the Holy Spirit, "But if the Spirit of Him who raised Jesus from the dead dwells in you, He who raised Christ from the dead will also give life to your mortal bodies through His Spirit who dwells in you" (Rom. 8:11).

Jesus is begging you to come to Him. Because He wants to set you free from your burdens. Listen carefully and you will hear Him saying, "I love you and My desire is to set you free from the afflictions that are holding you back." "I have come to give you an abundant life." The abundant life Christ wants to give you doesn't include an addiction to nicotine or anything else.

Being a child of God, ask yourself, why should I put-off this nicotine addiction? The answer is to bring glory to Christ, because He loves you and you love Him. Ask yourself two simple questions: how much does Jesus love me; and how did He show His love to me? Visualize your answer, by setting your eyes on the cross of Calvary. Jesus didn't die a horrible death on the cross for you to be in bondage to anything (cf. 1 Cor.6:12). The only power God desires us to be under is the power of His Holy Spirit. There are countless times when going through our hectic daily routines that we take God's love for granite, but everything we do should be wrapped up in the love of God.

God's love is a sacrificial love

Christ loves you sacrificially. Jesus willingly sacrificed His life on the cross, for you, even though He despised the shame of the cross. Without any thought for Himself, He freely gave His life in obedience to His Father's command. God's love is totally unselfish. However, He desires for you to put your faith in His son Jesus Christ for salvation. Jesus said, "Greater love has no one than this, than to lay down one's life for his friends" (John 15:13). Jesus laid down His life for you! Will you lay down your nicotine addiction for Him?

God's love is unconditional

Secondly, Christ loves us unconditionally. God's love has no strings attached to it. Speaking of the depth of God's love for His children, and how unconditionally He loves them is revealed in John 3:16, "For God so loved the world that He gave His only begotten Son, that whoever believes in Him should not parish but have everlasting life" (John 3:16).

God sent His son to die a horrible death on a cross, not because He wanted Him to die, but because He loves you and me that much, "God demonstrated His love toward us, in that while we were still sinners, Christ died for us" (Romans 5:8). God loves even sinners! It's that unconditional, sacrificial love that all of us need and crave. You can't find it in the things of this world. Only in Christ can that kind of unconditional love be realized. It's comforting to know that God loves us when we are unlovable. Even in our sinfulness God poured out His love upon us, "For when we were still without strength, in due time, Christ died for the ungodly" (Romans 5:6).

God's love is perfect

Thirdly, Christ is perfect. Therefore, His love is perfect. Jesus said in Matthew 5:48, "Therefore you shall be perfect, just as your Father in heaven is perfect" (Matthew 5:48).

The Apostle John wrote,

> Love has been perfected among us in this: that we may have boldness in the Day of Judgment; because as He is, so are we in this world. There is no fear in love; but perfect love casts out fear, because fear involves torment. But he who fears has not been made perfect in love. We love Him because He first loved us (1 John 4:17-19).

Whatever fears may be preventing you from quitting smoking, cast those fears off in the direction of the perfect love of Christ. We are made perfect, not on our own efforts, but by allowing God's love to live inside of us. God, as difficult as it might be to believe, is in the process of perfecting His perfect love in His children.

We are to become one with Christ, in love, while abiding in God through our love for Christ. Jesus said in Matthew 11:29 "Take my yoke upon you and learn from me." We are to be yoked together with Christ and united in love, with Him, for our heavenly Father. Jesus said, "...If anyone loves me, he will keep My word; and My Father will love him, and We will come to him and make our home with him" (John 14:23).

God's love for us and our love for His Son Jesus is what weaves us together as His family. It's this magnificent love of God that burns in our hearts and gives us the strength to "endure all things," the strength to "conquer all things," and gives us the strength that sets us free from anything that hinders our walk with Christ.

God's love is from the "Beginning of Time" to "The end of Time"

Finally, Christ has loved you from the very foundation of the world and He will love you until the end of this age, "Just as He chose us in Him before the foundation of the world, that we should be holy and without blame before Him in love" (Ephesians 1:4).

What does being holy and without blame mean to you? Think about how much God loves His son Jesus Christ. As much as the Father loves Jesus, He was willing to sacrifice Him in order to reconcile fallen humanity to Himself. I want to finish this chapter by having you read Romans 8:37-39. And after reading these verses, take a few moments to really meditate on the deepness of God's love for you. Then cast the burden of nicotine addiction or whatever else is burdening you into the midst of God's love and watch it disintegrate. God only wants good things for you!

> Yet in all these things we are more than conquerors through Him who loved us. For I am persuaded that neither death nor life, nor angels nor principalities nor powers, nor things present nor things to come, nor height nor depth, nor any other created thing, shall be able to separate us from the love of God which is in Christ Jesus our Lord (Rom. 8:37-39).

We truly are more than conquerors through Christ, and that includes conquering nicotine addiction. At this stage of your battle, it may seem impossible that you will be able to quit smoking. Don't be discouraged! I felt that way before I turned my addiction over to Christ. I have come to realize, and you will too, that nothing is impossible for God.

When we belong to Christ nothing can separate us from His love; except ourselves, through sinful behavior. Whether you are successful at putting-off smoking or not, God is still going to love you. God lusts for you to be free of anything that hinders the process of being like His son Jesus. We are given the authority, in the Scriptures, to put this addiction squarely on the shoulders of Christ (cf. Matthew 11:28-30). And through Christ's strength, we can be free.

There are many reasons why we should quit smoking and we make many excuses why we can't. I can assure you, with all sincerity, that everyone going through this process has the power, within themselves, through the indwelling of Christ, to quit smoking. If I can do it; you can do it. What I thought was impossible became possible through the love of Christ.

Chapter 9

PUTTING ON THE WHOLE ARMOR OF GOD EPHESIANS 6:10-17

Week five process and reading assignments:
Using the information you gathered from your put-off list (the unhealthy habits you have identified as put-offs) make a list beside them of the healthy habits you intend to put on in their place. Ask God to help you identify those areas.

Read Ephesians 6:10-17. Fill in the table below.

Name the six Pieces of Armor found in Ephesians 6:13-17	How can putting on that piece of armor help you remain smoke free?	When will you use this piece of armor to remain smoke free?

MEMORIZATION SCRIPTURES

"For the weapons of our warfare are not carnal but mighty in God for pulling down strongholds" (2 Cor. 10:4).

"Finally, my brothers, be strong in the Lord and in the power of His might. Put on the whole armor of God, that you may be able to stand against the wiles of the devil" (Ephesians 6:10-11).

INDIVIDUAL/SMALL GROUP QUESTIONS TO ANSWER THIS WEEK

1. How does smoking hurt your personal testimony for Christ?

2. How will quitting smoking help your personal testimony for Christ?

3. How can you use the Holy Spirit to strengthen you in times of weakness?

LESSON SIX

While thinking about putting on the "Whole Armor of God," the thought came to me. It's somewhat like preparing for a football game; both require protective armor. A Christian puts-on the Helmet of salvation; a football player puts-on head gear. A Christian puts-on the breastplate of righteousness; a football player puts-on his shoulder pads. A Christian wraps his waist in truth; a football player wraps his waist with padding. A Christian has their feet shod with the preparation of the gospel of peace; a football player wears cleats to keep himself from slipping.

The Christian walk and preparing for a football game are similar in that they both require certain disciplines: team work, self-discipline, perseverance, commitment, hard work, and sacrifice for others. The proper preparation and protective gear prepares a Christian to go onto the spiritual battlefield confident of victory.

I hope you realize that you are going through a spiritual battle. When one of God's children attempts to accomplish something that pleases the Lord, like breaking the head-lock the devil has on them through addiction, there will always be a spiritual battle to fight. And like a football player the Christian's preparation and armor is not to keep them out of the battle, but to protect them while in the midst of the battle. You can't go into a spiritual battle naked and unprepared any more than a football player can go on the football field without his protective gear. If you do, you will end up torn, tattered, and discouraged. How do we prepare ourselves for these spiritual battles? Ephesians 6:10-17 describes, in detail, how to protect ourselves during a spiritual battle,

> Finally, my brethren, be strong in the Lord and in the power of His might. **"Put-on"** the whole armor of God that you may be able to stand against the wiles of the devil. For we do not wrestle against flesh and blood, but against principalities, against powers, against the rulers of the darkness of this age, against spiritual *hosts* of wickedness in the heavenly *places*. Therefore take up the whole armor of God that you may be able to withstand in the evil day, and having done all, to stand. Stand therefore, having girded your waist with truth, having put on the breastplate of righteousness, and having shod your feet with the preparation of the gospel of peace; above all, taking the shield of faith with which you will be able to quench all the fiery darts of the wicked one. And take

the helmet of salvation, and the sword of the Spirit, which is the word of God (Eph. 6:10-17 emphasis mine). (Notice Paul's instruction to **"put-on"** which is how a Christian changes through the process of renewing the mind)

Paul's instructions are to put-on protective gear, to stand firm, to be ready, to be prepared, and to cover your head with salvation: the "Blood of Christ." Football games are just games. They are not a matter of life and death, but the spiritual battle you are fighting is a matter of life and breath. The apostle Paul wrote that our battles are not carnal but spiritual. Unlike football games we don't fight against another person. Although it seems like it at times, but that is another lie from Satan. If Satan can get you focused on someone else and off of him; he's winning the battle. Our fight is against "principalities," "against powers," "against the rulers of darkness," and "against spiritual hosts of wickedness in heavenly places" (cf. Ephesians 6:12).

We need to put-on the complete armor of God in order to prevail against the tricks of the devil. We often fight against ourselves doubting the victories we can achieve through the power of the Holy Spirit. Doubt and discouragement are two of Satan's most effective tools. We need to stay focused on the battle, at hand, not on ourselves or others. Paul gives us a put-on list on how to prepare ourselves for the spiritual battles to come.

Put-on truth

The first piece of armor on Paul's list is from verse 14, which says, "Stand therefore, having girded you waist with truth." Girded in this verse literally means to tuck in your waist band and get ready to fight. That's what an athlete did in Jesus' day right before an athletic event. We are instructed to tuck in and wrap around our waste truth. What is the truth we need to be equipped with? The truth Paul is talking about is revealed in the Gospel of John.

Jesus said, "I am the way, the truth, and the life no one comes to the Father except through me" (John 14:6).

When we gird ourselves with truth we are wrapping ourselves in one truth. That truth being, Jesus Christ is the only remedy for sin and the only way to get to heaven. Contrary to secular beliefs, the Bible is clear, that faith in Jesus Christ is the only way to escape separation from God for all eternity, "For there is one God and one mediator between God and man, the man Jesus Christ" (1 Timothy 2:5).

Breastplate of righteousness

The next armor on Paul's list is putting-on the breastplate of righteousness, "For He made Him who knew no sin to be sin for us, that we might become the righteousness of God in Him" (2 Corinthians 5:21). Who credits His righteousness to us? It's the Lord Jesus. When we accept Christ as Lord and savior, we are putting-on the righteousness of Christ. According to the teachings of this Scripture, we wrap ourselves with the truth of Christ and we put on the righteousness of Christ.

Being shod with the gospel of peace

The next piece of armor to put-on is from verse 15, which says, "Having shod your feet with the preparation of the gospel of peace." What is the gospel? It's the good news of Jesus Christ: accepting by faith the death and resurrection of Christ on the cross for the forgiveness of our sins and putting our faith in Him for eternal life. That is the good news! Paul is telling us to be prepared to share the good news of Christ with others while in the midst of the battle. Satan often uses our times of spiritual warfare to distract us from sharing the good news of Christ. Under any circumstances, share with anyone and everyone that God brings into your sphere of influence this wonderful news of salvation available to them through saving faith in Christ.

If you think real hard, you'll arrive at the conclusion that you can't put your hope in anything that is of this world: jobs, money, retirement accounts, political leaders, governments, etc. All have been proven to be at the whim of fallen humanity. The only true hope, in this life, is in the promises of Jesus, and the life to come. Wrap the good news of Christ around your feet and take it everywhere you go.

Shield of faith

Paul further instructs us to take up the shield of faith in order to quench the fiery darts of the devil. Who do we put our faith in? And where does our faith come from? Romans 3:22-25,

> Even the righteousness of God through "faith" in Jesus Christ, to all and on all who believe for there is no difference; for all have sinned and fall short of the glory of God, being justified freely by His grace through the redemption that is in Christ Jesus." Whom God set forth as propitiation (substitute) through "faith," to demonstrate His righteousness, because God had passed over the sins that were previously committed (emphasis mine).

These Scriptures teach us that we are to put our faith in Christ. And that the very faith we possess comes from God! Paul wrote to the Romans, "…to think soberly, as God has dealt to each one a measure of faith" (Romans 12:3).

Helmet of salvation

The final two pieces of armor Paul instructs us to attire ourselves with are "The Helmet of Salvation" and "The Sword of the Spirit." Before you read further examine yourself to see if you are in the faith. Ask yourself these questions: have I accepted the

Lord Jesus Christ for the forgiveness of my sins; trusting in Him for salvation? Have I given Him permission to take up residence in my heart, and to be the lord of my life? Allowing Jesus to be the Lord of your life is important because we all serve something or someone; let it be Christ. If you have never given your life to Christ or need to recommit your life to Him simply pray these words in the name Jesus: I'm sorry for my sins, please forgive me of my sins, come into my heart, and be the lord of my life. Amen!

The sword of the Spirit

The last piece of armor on Paul's list is "The sword of the spirit," which is the word of God" (cf. Ephesians 6:17). "For the word of God is living and powerful, and sharper than any two-edged sword, piercing even to the division of soul and spirit, and of joints and marrow, and is a discerner of the thoughts and intents of the heart" (Hebrews 4: 12).

Who is this "Living Word?" The Apostle John proclaims who the "Living Word" is in John 1:1, "In the beginning was the Word and the Word was with God and the Word was God." In verse 14 John writes, "And the word became flesh and dwelt among us and we beheld His glory as the only begotten of the Father, full of grace and truth" (John 1:1, 14). The book of Hebrews tells us that the Word of God is alive, it's powerful, and it's able to pull down any strongholds in our lives.

It's critical for you to understand the power available to you in the Scriptures. John clearly identifies Jesus as the Living Word. The Bible is the inspired Word of God. Inspired, meaning, breathed out, spoken by the very breath of God (cf. 2 Tim. 3:16). My hope is that your understanding is that when you pick up the Bible you are holding the very essence of the Lord Jesus in your hands. Jesus is alive! He's powerful! It's His spoken Word that each one of us needs to live a victorious Christian life. Not a life of bondage, but a life full of hope and victories over the things that keep us from being everything God has ordained us to be.

I believe the most important part of a Christian's life is to embrace the teachings of the Bible, with all their heart, soul, mind, and strength. Absorbing, like a sponge, every breathed out word of God in the Scriptures. No other Christian discipline will enable you to grow spiritually more than embracing the Word of God. When you hold that Bible in your hand let it to do what God has sent it out to do: giving new life to those who desperately need it. God's word will always accomplish what He has sent it out to do,

> So shall My word be that goes forth from My
> mouth;It shall not return to Me void,
> But it shall accomplish what I please,
> And it shall prosper *in the thing* for which I sent it.
> (Isaiah 55:11 italics theirs)

Let's review this week's lesson. We are to put on the truth of Christ, the righteousness of Christ, be prepared with the good news of Christ, put our faith in Christ, obtain our salvation in Christ, and grab a hold of the word of God, which is Christ. What is Paul telling us? My answer to that question is that we need to be covered from the top of our head to the very soles of our feet with the Lord Jesus. "But put on the Lord Jesus Christ, and make no provision for the flesh, to *fulfill its* lusts" (Romans 13:14 italics theirs) It's the covering of Christ that enables us to be victorious in the spiritual battles that are sure to come our way. When the devil strolls up to you and sees that you are covered from head to toe with Jesus he can't do anything but shake his head and flee (cf. James 4:7). You already have the victory! You received that when you became a Christian. Put-on the whole armor of God, and you can't be defeated.

Utilizing the put-off and put-on doctrine of change from Ephesians 4:22-24 and applying it to Ephesians 6:13-17,

- We put off the lies of Satan and put on the truth found in God's Word.
- We put off our sinfulness and put on the righteousness of Jesus.
- We put off doubt and fear and put on the Gospel of Jesus Christ through the "Shield of Faith."
- We put off condemnation and put on the "Helmet of Salvation."
- We put off the clutter, in our minds, of this world and replace it with the peace that comes from the "Sword of the Spirit" which is the "Word of God."

Jesus is our armor, and it's only through putting-on Christ that we can overcome the wickedness of this world. A Christian's goal in life should always be to please God. And we please God by being like His son Jesus Christ (cf. Matt. 3:17, 2 Cor. 5:9).

I want to challenge you to take the things Paul listed in Ephesians 6:13-17 and examine them to see where there might be weaknesses in your armor. When we are obedient to God's word and apply those principles to our lives. We will find victory. Nicotine addiction was one of the scariest and hardest battles I have faced in my Christian life. Through that struggle I came to realize one thing and that was to put my trust totally in the hands of the Lord. Believing that with God in my corner I couldn't fail. God promises that nothing will be impossible for you (cf. Philippians 4:13).

I got great news for you! Jesus Christ wins the battle!!!

Chapter 10

PERSEVERANCE NEHEMIAH CHAPTERS 4&6

WEEK SIX PROCESS AND READING ASSIGNMENTS

Continue to work on the put-off and put-on list. Be diligent preparing this list!

Read Nehemiah Chapters 4 & 6 and answer these questions,

1. How did Nehemiah demonstrate perseverance?

2. How can you demonstrate perseverance in your own life?

3. How will the ability to persevere help you be successful in putting-off nicotine addiction?

MEMORIZATION SCRIPTURES

"Indeed we count them blessed who endure. You have heard of the perseverance of Job and seen the end intended by the Lord—that the Lord is very compassionate and merciful" (James 5:11).

"To knowledge self-control, to self-control perseverance, to perseverance godliness…" (2 Peter 1:6).

INDIVIDUAL/SMALL GROUP QUESTIONS TO ANSWER THIS WEEK

1. How did Jesus persevere?

2. How have you persevered in the past?

3. Why would quitting smoking please God?

LESSON SEVEN

How many of you have found that living the Christian life is easy? Doing the right thing and living for Christ is challenging. Have there been times in your Christian walk when you felt like giving up? Maybe you heard yourself telling God that it's just too demanding?

Doing the things that please God takes steadfastness and perseverance. Throughout the centuries many Christian's have struggled to do the right thing. That's not a new concept. Even the Apostle Paul had his struggles. Romans 7:18-25,

> For I know that in me (that is, in my flesh) nothing good dwells; for to will is present with me, but how to perform what is good I do not find. For the good that I will to do, I do not do; but the evil I will not to do, that I practice. Now if I do what I will not to

do, it is no longer I who do it, but sin that dwells in me. I find then a law, that evil is present with me, the one who wills to do good. For I delight in the law of God according to the inward man. But I see another law in my members, warring against the law of my mind, and bringing me into captivity to the law of sin which is in my members. O wretched man that I am! Who will deliver me from this body of death? I thank God—through Jesus Christ our Lord! So then, with the mind I myself serve the law of God, but with the flesh the law of sin (emphasis theirs).

The apostle Paul wrestled with this same question: why is it so hard to do the right thing? Did the other apostles struggle? Peter denied Jesus three times. Doubting Thomas said, "Unless I see in His hands the print of the nails, and put my finger into the print of the nails, and put my hand into His side, I will not believe" (John 20:25).

Everybody struggles at times. Peter is the rock Jesus said He would build His church on. Thomas was the one who bragged that he was willing to die with Jesus. All fled at Jesus' arrest.

What would the Lord Jesus say to you in times of struggles? He probably would remind you of a Scripture, "I can do all things through Christ who strengthens me?" (Philippians 4:13). Get in a quiet place and listen real close. You will hear Him say, "Fear not, it is I." We need to fight through times of doubt and pain. Past failures can cripple you, if you let them: all the times you failed Jesus, failed others, and failed yourself. Take Paul's advice from Philippians, "Brethren, I do not count myself to have apprehended; but one thing *I* do, forgetting those things which are behind and reaching forward to those things which are ahead, I press toward the goal for the prize of the upward call of God in Christ Jesus" (Philippians 3:13-14 italics theirs).

Isn't that perseverance? Forgetting past failures and pressing on! The Holy Spirit is saying to you, "Don't stop trying," "Don't give up," "Don't quit when you are so close to victory." So many people give up right before experiencing victory. Don't be one of those people. Keep your eyes focused on Jesus and never give up.

One of the main ingredients in living a victorious Christian life is perseverance. The Holman Bible Dictionary said this about perseverance, "Maintaining Christian faith through trying times of life. This idea is inherent throughout the N.T. in the great interplay of the themes of assurance and warning." - Holman Bible Dictionary

What are some things the Bible implies that we need to persevere through? Here's a short list: evil, temptation, false teaching, hard times, draught and famine, sin, trials, persecutions. Can you think of some others? Every aspect of the Christian life revolves around perseverance: hanging onto your faith no matter what circumstances surround you. God has given us this gift of perseverance. Along with that gift He has given us everything we need to live a victorious Christian life in Christ.

Nehemiah was given a gigantic task to rebuild the walls around Jerusalem. Even though he had the blessing of the king, there were enemies all around trying to discourage him and keep him from completing the task. Nehemiah persevered through their threats. He was able to rebuild the walls around Jerusalem in just fifty-two days.

There were several familiar qualities Nehemiah demonstrated that we should already be familiar with:

1. Nehemiah prayed before He began the task God set before him.
2. Nehemiah and his fellow workers were committed to each other and committed to finishing the work at hand.
3. Nehemiah and his workers kept a lookout for the enemy and armed themselves for battle.
4. Nehemiah trusted in the strength of the Lord, not in his own strength.
5. Nehemiah had a plan and he stuck with it.

6. Nehemiah, even though his life was threatened, ignored the treats and the lies of the enemy and pressed on.

There is much we can learn from Nehemiah's experience that will help us in this fight to be nicotine free: have a plan, trust in Christ, don't give up, commit to the process, don't be discouraged by others who want to see you fail.

How do we develop perseverance?

1. Spiritual growth.
2. Fruitfulness.
3. Putting on God's armor.
4. Through God's chastening.

Spiritual growth

In order to grow in our spiritual lives we need to speak the truth in love, "But, speaking the truth in love may grow up in all things into Him who is the head—Christ..." (Ephesians 4:15). Growing into Christ-likeness doesn't happen overnight. It's a process called progressive sanctification. We need to grow-up spiritually: from a baby drinking milk to a mature Christian eating meat. For us to put-off that old man and put-on Jesus it's imperative we speak the truth to ourselves, to God, and to others.

From what we've learned so far, what does being honest to ourselves really mean? The meaning must be interpreted as coming out of denial, admitting our powerlessness, and trusting Christ to set us free. Scripture instructs us to "Grow up in all things; into Him who is the head--Christ (cf. Ephesians 4:15). In all things, what does that mean? The apostle Paul wrote, "When I was a child, I spoke as a child, I understood as a child, I thought as a child; but when I became a man, I put away childish things" (1 Corinthians 13:11).

Is smoking a childish thing? Ask yourself why did I start smoking in the first place? Was it to impress your peers or to fit in with a certain crowd? Did you start smoking because you thought it was cool? Are those childish reasons? Take some time and make a list of grown-up reasons why you should quit smoking.

The signs of true spiritual growth are how much are you becoming like Christ on a daily basis. Are you more like Christ this year than last? Are you more like Christ today than you were yesterday? These are great question to ask yourself in order to measure your spiritual growth. It's scriptural to examine ourselves and evaluate where we are in our relationship with the Lord (cf. Lamentations. 3:40).

Did Jesus persevere through temptations and persecutions (cf. Luke 4:1-13)? Yes, Jesus persevered all the way to His death on the cross. We too are expected to persevere in order to overcome. Even to death if necessary (cf. Revelation 12:11). If you could ask Jesus what He thought about smoking what do you think His answer would be? Meditate on these questions. Am I more like Christ today then yesterday? Am I more like Christ this year than last? What goals have I set, for myself, to grow more like Jesus?

Fruitfulness

To measure our spiritual maturity there needs to be signs of spiritual fruitfulness. What are the signs of spiritual growth? Answer. The "Fruit of the Spirit," shining through us. Fruit of the Spirit being singular in its meaning. You receive all nine manifestations of the spirit at the same time. Evidence of these fruits is a sign of maturity in our spiritual growth. Seeing the Fruit of the Spirit manifested in our lives attest to ourselves and to others that we are becoming more like Christ. "But the fruit of the Spirit is love, joy, peace, longsuffering, kindness, goodness, faithfulness gentleness, self-control. Against such there is no law" (Galatians 5:22-23).

How do we become fruitful and how do we continue to be

fruitful? In the Gospel of John, Jesus instructs us on where to become fruitful and how to remain fruitful. John 15: 4-8,

> Abide in Me, and I in you. As the branch cannot bear fruit of itself, unless it abides in the vine, neither can you, unless you abide in Me. "I am the vine, you are the branches. He who abides in Me, and I in him, bears much fruit; for without Me you can do nothing. If anyone does not abide in Me, he is cast out as a branch and is withered; and they gather them and throw them into the fire, and they are burned. If you abide in Me, and My words abide in you, you will ask what you desire, and it shall be done for you. By this My Father is glorified, that you bear much fruit; so you will be My disciples.

We remain fruitful by abiding in Jesus Christ. When we allow ourselves to be separated from Him we quickly become unfruitful. All of us have tried to do things apart from Christ, and what happens? We fail. But we don't give up; we persevere by returning to the vine. We remain in the vine by living out the biblical disciplines. The last "Fruit of the Spirit" is self-control. Recall the biblical disciplines from week two (cf. chapter 5): Bible study and meditation, praying continuously, staying in fellowship, and serving Christ.

Put-on God's armor

Review last week's teaching on putting-on
the whole armor of God.

Through God's chastening

Finally, we persevere through the chastening of the Lord. God disciplines us because we are His children, "The LORD disciplines those he loves, as a father the son he delights in" (Proverbs 3:12). God delights in teaching us how to grow into the image of His son Jesus (cf. Rom. 8:29). I have felt the chastening of the Lord on occasion since becoming a Christian. None of us are perfect, and we all need to be corrected at times. If you haven't already felt God giving you an attitude adjustment I'm sure you will experience that along the way. When we learn the lessons God wants to teach us, He picks us up, wipes us off, and continues the process of growing us into the likeness of His son.

And what happens if we don't learn those lessons? We stray away from the vine and end up going through the same old struggles over and over again until we finally surrender it all to Christ. Jesus cautioned us that trials would come our way and He warned us of the animosity the world would have toward Jesus' followers (cf. John 15:18-19). Satan's desire is to separate you from the vine: getting you isolated. Remaining in the vine, protects us, teaches us, comforts us, and grows us into the image of Jesus.

Remind yourself daily that you are not of this world. Solidify, in your heart, that smoking is an addictive resource robbing habit that is stealing years from your life and service to Christ. You can't play at being a Christian. You must be sold out one-hundred percent to living a life for Christ (cf. Rev 3:16). No holding back! Jesus, I'm yours, and I'm trusting in you to fill me every day with that living water that flows from heaven. Jesus when speaking to the Samaritan woman said, "If you knew the gift of God, and who it is who says to you, "Give me a drink" you would have asked Him, and He would have given you living water" (John 4:10). In order to live a victorious Christian life we must take to heart what John the Baptist broadcast for all to hear, "Jesus must increase, but I must decrease" (John 3:30). Dying to self and living for Christ is a sure indicator that we are on the right path to spiritual maturity.

Since we are learning how to persevere, this would be a good time to discuss relapses, and how to avoid them. The first step in preventing a relapse is to realize that you are going to be tempted to smoke. And it's important for you to be prepared to resist that temptation. Temptation, of itself, is not a sin. The act of taking action on the temptation is where sin gets a foothold. Jesus was tempted in the wilderness, but didn't sin. He used the most powerful weapon He knew to combat the temptations Satan presented to Him. Jesus used the "Word of God" to repel the devils lies (cf. Matthew 4:1-11).

Satan can only place the temptation before you, it's up to you to take the bait or refuse it. Utilizing the Word of God, in times of temptation, is our best weapon. Working diligently on the biblical principles in this book will help in preparing you to recognize the tricks of the devil. And will give you some tools to use that will make the devil sprint away from you as fast as he can run (cf. James 4:7).

Keep in mind, just because you have relapsed doesn't mean you have to give-up. It just means you've had a setback. During the tough times is when perseverance pays off. A relapse doesn't mean you've lost the war. It only means you've lost one battle in a long war. Victory can be just around the bend. Here are some things to be on the lookout for that can cause a relapse:

- Being around other smokers: avoid familiar places and those who are still smokers.
- Drinking alcohol: avoid alcohol which lessens your resolve to quit.
- Being over confident: keep in mind that it's through the Lord's strength we are able to overcome not our own strength.
- Becoming isolated from your accountability or support team: be diligent in staying in contact with your support team.
- Not getting enough rest: when you are tired your resistance is lessened. This is a time when the enemy will try to convince you that a cigarette will give you energy. Don't fall for that lie.

- Stress: avoid stressful situations as much as possible. The devil will work hard at creating stressful situations at work and at home. Be on the lookout for his tricks!
- Anger, self-pity, and a negative attitude: be positive and control your anger: "Be angry and sin not" recognize unrighteous anger for what it is, a sin, and a tool the enemy uses to discourage you and get you off track.
- Don't be self-destructive: maintain a positive attitude throughout this process. Visualize yourself as a non-smoker and find joy in embracing all the positive things that will come to you and your family as a non-smoker.

If you do experience a relapses, don't give up, "persevere;" keep on fighting. Repent of your sin, pick yourself up, brush yourself off, and get back in the fight.

Chapter 11

MAINTAINING A SMOKE FREE LIFE

WEEK SEVEN PROCESS AND READING ASSIGNMENT

Read Romans chapter eight and meditate on its meaning. Answer the question, why is it so important for me to cast-off the things of the flesh and walk in the spirit?

MEMORIZATION SCRIPTURES

"For those who live according to the flesh set their minds on the things of the flesh, but those who live according to the spirit, the things of the spirit" (Romans 8:5).

"You shall love the Lord your God with all your heart, with all your soul, with all your mind, and with all your strength. This is the first commandment" (Mark 12:30).

INDIVIDUAL/SMALL GROUP QUESTIONS TO ANSWER THIS WEEK

1. Have I established a strong accountability team? Y____ N____?
2. Do I have a plan in place to help me maintain a healthy life style? Y___ N___?

3. What is my plan? Write out a plan of action that will help you maintain a healthy life style which should include an exercise plan, healthy eating habits, an accountability team, regular prayer, Bible reading and meditation, Christian fellowship, and service to Christ.

FINAL LESSON

As we begin our final lesson in this process of off putting-off nicotine addiction I want to encourage you to diligently meditate on what it means to walk in the spirit and not in the flesh. The process of putting-off fleshly desires and putting-on the desires of the Spirit will be crucial in putting-off old sinful habits and putting-on new Christ honoring habits.

Before we come to know Christ, whether we want to admit it or not, the desires of our heart was to satisfy the flesh (nicotine addiction satisfies the flesh). The Scriptures teach us that after accepting Christ for the forgiveness of our sins we are buried with Jesus in the grave, "crucifying the flesh." After our ceremonial burial, we are born again a new spiritual person: having the Spirit of God take up residence inside of us, "Therefore if anyone is in Christ he is a new creation old things have passed away; behold all things have become new" (2 Cor. 5:17).

This new birth begins the process of putting-off the old corrupted man (fleshly desires) and putting-on the new man: desiring the things of the Spirit. This new birth will become evident by the way we live our lives. Confirming the Spirit of Christ is working in us as we begin to manifest the godly attributes that are listed in Galatians 5:22-24.

God promises us a new heart upon our conversion. The Holy Spirit living in us transforms a hardened heart, full of sin, into a heart that seeks the things of God. What a transformation! The power of the Holy Spirit can raise the dead, move Mountains, heal the sick, and cast out demons; but the true miracles of the indwelling of the Holy Spirit are changed lives.

The redeemed of God should be children of humility, forsaking the desires of the flesh and offering up to God a broken and contrite heart always striving to please Him by pursuing the things of the Spirit: love, joy, peace, longsuffering, kindness, goodness, faithfulness, gentleness, and self-control (cf. Galatians 5:22-23). Developing these spiritual fruits 24/7 will bring you into a closer relationship with Christ than you could ever imagine, "Those who are Christ's have crucified the flesh with its passions and desires. If we live in the Spirit let us also walk in the Spirit" (Gal.5:24-25).

As you battle to be nicotine free, hold on to this thought, "YOU" are a child of the creator of the whole universe. "YOU" are a joint heir with Christ and entitled to all the promises of the Scriptures. The transformation from children of the prince of this world to being transformed into the children of the Redeemed is the greatest miracle of all!

COMMITMENT PAGE

In addition to putting together plans to stay smoke free read and sign this commitment page. There's something about signing your name to a plan of action that prompts you to stick with it.

I, (name) _____ on (date)_____ in order to continue to please God in all areas of my life commit to remaining smoke free and when tempted to smoke I will put-on the full armor of God and do battle against this giant of nicotine addiction. I will continue to rely on the Holy Spirit to lead me to victory. When being tempted to smoke, I will call one of my accountability partners before the temptation gets too strong. I will follow my plan of action and remain faithful to it for as long as it takes to be totally and completely smoke free.

Signature_____

In order to maintain a smoke free lifestyle it's important to take action steps after completing this process. I strongly recommend that you remain in fellowship with those in your small group. If you went through this process on your own find a support group in your community, and stay in contact with your trusted friend. Many local hospitals have smoking cessation classes. Check to see if there are any Christ-centered smoking cessation programs in your community. Getting involved in a recovery program like Celebrate Recovery can help tremendously. Even if they don't have a nicotine addictions small group many of them have life choice small groups.

1.800. QUIT.NOW www.eguitnow.com is a great source of information that can help you stay tobacco free. Hank Williams Jr., in a country song, called "Old Habits" sang, "I used life savers to get off cigarettes." My brother-in-law Larry used chewing on tooth picks to help him quit.

Use every resource available to you if it will help you and not harm you or others.

Don't let your guard down! Your enemy is not going to easily relinquish the hold he had on you. The battle has really just begun, but you have the strength, power, and the right weapons to defeat this giant of nicotine addiction. Recall the Scriptures you memorized and add to them. Review the lessons in this book regularly. Work your put-on list, read Scripture, pray, contact an accountability partner, exercise; listen to praise music.

THE IMPORTANCE OF CHANGING ROUTINES

After being on vacation for a week, I prepared myself to go back to the factory. I had a week under my belt of being smoke free and I was feeling pretty good about myself. On the first break of the day I went out to the smoking area to see some of my smoker friends to tell them the great news that I had quit smoking. What a mistake that was! The smoking area was filled with smoke; it took my breath away. I realized I couldn't do that on breaks anymore. I understood, at that moment, I needed to change my routine. I also had a habit of reaching in my shirt pocket for a cigarette. After doing that several times, a light went off in my head. I had the idea to put a pocket Bible in my shirt pocket and every time I reached for a cigarette, instead of a cigarette, I was reminded of God's Word. I used that little Bible to change what I did on breaks. I found a quiet place to read the Scriptures. The time I spent in the Scriptures, at work each day, really helped me get the Word of God into my heart. Be creative when it comes to avoiding familiar places and people that remind you of smoking. Someday you will be strong enough to be in those situations without being tempted to smoke. Take some time and make a list of things you can do instead of the same old routines.

One of the results of my quitting smoking was that I gained 30 pounds. This caught me by surprise. Before I knew it, I had to buy larger sized jeans. Eating healthier foods and exercise is recommended to help you maintain a smoke free lifestyle. Most hospitals and many health clubs have information on low-cost healthy foods. Use whatever resources that are available to you to be a healthier you. Gaining weight is one of the excuses many people use to avoid quitting smoking, and can be a key ingredient in relapses. The fear of gaining weight is a form of denial. With the proper information and persistent effort you can be a non-smoker and maintain a healthy weight. Here are two secure government web-sites that have a lot of good information on eating healthier. https://www.nutrition.gov/   https://www.choosemyplate.gov/MyPlate

Exercise is a great tool to use in your battle to remain smoke free. And at the same time help you maintain your desirable weight. Exercise relaxes you and gives you a feeling of accomplishment. Walking is one of the best exercises you can do. Upper body stretching exercises are a great way to relax and relieve tension. Deep breathing exercises are great to use in stressful situations especially when you are tied to a desk and unable get away. You can also use deep breathing exercises while sitting on your couch, driving down the road, or whenever you feel stressed. Stress is a strong trigger and another cause of relapse. Be on the lookout, the enemy will manufacture stressful situations trying to get you to smoke again.

Remember you're in a spiritual battle and that battle will continue to rage even after you have quit smoking. The devil is not happy about the freedom you have found from tobacco use. There are going to be times of temptation especially when you are in a stressful situation (cf. chapter 10 on relapse). You can't give in! There were times after I quit smoking that I just had to stand firm: stomping my foot on the ground and saying, **"NO,"** "**I am not going to smoke."** The devil is going to come after you when you quit smoking; you can count on it. He's certainly not happy about you breaking free of one of the most destructive strongholds available to him.

I had been smoke free for a week. I woke-up that Monday morning feeling pretty good about my freedom from smoking. Showered, ate breakfast, and headed out the door for work. A few months before I quit smoking I bought a new Ford ranger with flair sides; it was beautiful. I was fifty-one years old at the time and that was the first new vehicle I had ever owned.

Lunch and morning coffee in hand I headed out the door. As I approached my truck, in the bed was the ugliest, burnt orange colored, bull dogged faced dog I had ever seen. He was growling and scratching the back of the cab and up and down the sides of the bed. I was shocked, scared, and at a loss for what to do. I tried to run the dog off, but it continued its rampage of growling and scratching the truck. The more I tried to get the dog to leave the crazier it acted. I set my coffee and lunch bag down. Sprinted to the house and grabbed an 835 Mossberg pump 12 gauge shotgun from the gun safe. I loaded the shotgun with 12 gauge 00 buckshot shells, and raced outside. To my surprise, the dog was out of the truck and standing in the yard. Cautiously, I walked over to where the dog was. Placing the shotgun on my shoulder I pointed it directly at its wrinkled face, but didn't pull the trigger. I often wonder, even today, why I didn't pull that trigger. The dog finally left. What a stressful situation the devil had manufactured for me that morning. Sadly that was just one of many more to come. Talk about a "hound from your worst nightmare" that was it.

Guess what I craved after that encounter. With hands trembling, I wanted a cigarette so bad I could taste it. Later I was so jubilant that I didn't have any cigarettes anywhere in the house or in the truck. Get rid of **all** cigarettes and smoking paraphernalia in your house, car, office, or wherever you spent time smoking.

I returned the shotgun to the gun safe and went to work. By the grace of God I didn't smoke that day. However, my beautiful Ford Ranger was all scratched up. It took all of my willpower to hold back the tears on the drive to work that morning and several days after. But the important thing was that I was still nicotine free.

That was the meanest looking dog I have ever seen in my life. I know, in the confines of my heart, the devil sent that dog to stress me out, trying to get me to smoking again. It almost worked. I tell this story to emphasize the fact that Satan is going to stand against you in ways you would never expect (cf. 1 Chronicles.21:1). Expect the unexpected. Put-on the "Whole Armor of God" and get yourself girded up for the battle. Be mean, be tough, be persistent, and don't give in an inch to the devil's tricks, "Yet in all these things we are more than conquerors through Him who loved us" (Rom. 8:37).

CONCLUSION

Congratulations! Unless you are one of those people who read the end of the book before the beginning, I assume, you have completed the process set forth in this book. My prayer is that you have joined the community of non-smokers. To the best of my ability, I have tried to write a common since, Christ honoring, smoking cessation process based on biblical principles to assist God's people in putting-off nicotine addiction. I hope the biblical principles in this book will help you deal with all of life's problems in a Christ honoring way. I want to encourage those who were successful in putting-off the habit of smoking to continue to stand steadfast in this fight and don't give in an inch to our enemy. Don't allow him an area in your life to sneak back in. Be on the lookout for his schemes. I want all of you to know I am proud of you for listening to the Lord's leading and persevering through this process.

Even if you were not able to quit smoking, I urge you to continue working this process and when the time is right you will be successful in becoming a non-smoker. Hang in there! Cling to the Lord! Be persistent in prayer! Absorb the Word of God! Eventually you will be successful. Quitting smoking is a battle, but it won't always be so hard. The day will come when you will no longer desire a cigarette. You may lose a battle or two but the war will be won through the power of Christ.

My prayer for you,

> Rejoice in the Lord always. Again I will say, rejoice! Let your gentleness be known to all men. The Lord *is* at hand. Be anxious for nothing, but in everything by prayer and supplication, with thanksgiving, let your requests be made known to God; and the peace of God, which surpasses all understanding, will guard your hearts and minds through Christ Jesus (Phil. 4:4-7 italics theirs)

> God bless you all!!!

> My Prayers are with you!!!

BIBLIOGRAPHY

A Report from the Surgeon General. *www.cdc.gov.* May 2015. http://www.cdc.gov/tobacco/data_statistics/fact_sheets/health_effects/effects_cig_smoking/ (accessed June 2015).

American Cancer Society. *www.lung.org.* 2014. http://www.lung.org/stop-smoking/about-smoking/facts-figures/general-smoking-facts.html-2014 (accessed December 06, 2014).

American Lung Association. *www.lung.org.* March 2015. http://www.lung.org/stop-smoking/smoking-facts/e-cigarettes-and-lung-health.html (accessed August 2015).

Baker, John. *Celebrate Recovery.* Grand Rapids: Zondervan, 1998.

Blakeslee, Sandra. "New York Times Magazine." *www.nytimes.com.* March 29, 1987. http://www.nytimes.com/1987/03/29/magazine/nicotine-harder-to-kickthan-heroin.html?pagewanted=all (accessed March 01, 2018).

Deemer, Dr. Lori. *Rising From the Ashes.* PowerPoint, Greenfield: Brandywine Community Church, 2015, all.

Donald H. Taylo Jr, Ph. D., Vic Hasselblad, Ph.D, et al. Hd.r,. "Benefits of Smoking Cessation for Longevity." *American Journal of Public Health* 92, no. 6 (June 2002).

Gerry Oster, et al. "The ecomomic cost of smoking and benefits of quitting for individual smokers." *Science Direct* 13, no. 4 (June 1984): 377-389.

Holman Bible Dictionary. *Holman Illustrated Bible Dictionary.* Nashville: Holman Bible Publishers, 2003.

Kannel, William B. "Update on the role of cigarette smoking in coronary artery disease." *American Heart Journal* 101, no. 4 (March 1981): 319-328.

Mattiias Oberg, Ph.D, Mrritta S. Jaakkola, Ph.D., et al. "Worldwide Burden of Disease from Exposure to Second-hand Smoke." *The Lancet* 377, no. 9760 (January 2011): 139-146.